GREAT GOURMET

EXCITING, GRATIFYING, ~~~~~~~~~~~~~~~
are the words for this wonderful book which
will put new fragrance and flavor into your cooking!

You can surprise and delight your family and friends
with rare and succulent meals that can even
be served to children, since when wine is cooked it
contains no alcohol—but serves to
enhance and enrich the flavor of fine food.

Myra Waldo, world traveler and author of numerous
cook books, here gives you all kinds of ways
to increase the pleasures of your table!

THE COMPLETE BOOK OF WINE COOKERY

MYRA WALDO

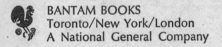

BANTAM BOOKS
Toronto/New York/London
A National General Company

THE COMPLETE BOOK OF WINE COOKERY

A Bantam Cookbook Shelf edition/published October 1965

2nd printing ......June 1966	7th printing .....April 1970
3rd printing ......June 1967	8th printing ......May 1970
4th printing ....August 1968	9th printing ......Feb. 1971
5th printing ......Sept. 1969	10th printing ......Oct. 1971
6th printing ....Dec. 1969	11th printing ......Feb. 1972

Revised edition published February 1973

Library of Congress Catalog Card Number: 65-11849

Published simultaneously in the United States and Canada

Bantam Books are published by Bantam Books, Inc., a National
General company. Its trade-mark, consisting of the words "Bantam
Books" and the portrayal of a bantam, is registered in the United
States Patent Office and in other countries. Marca Registrada.
Bantam Books, Inc., 666 Fifth Avenue, New York, N.Y. 10019.

Printed in the United States of America

CONTENTS

THE COMPLETE BOOK OF WINE COOKERY

INTRODUCTION

A half century ago, comparatively few Americans traveled abroad, but in the past decade, hundreds of thousands have toured Europe. At first, they visited only the capital cities; later, American tourists hired autos and drove through the smallest villages and hamlets of each country, exploring, sightseeing, eating the local dishes and drinking the local wines as they went. Once home, they missed having wine with their meals in the European style, and also yearned for the more sophisticated taste of foods prepared with wine.

Thus, the past several years have seen a tremendous surge of interest in this country in gourmet cooking, particularly in foreign dishes, and in wine-drinking. Not so very long ago, a guest invited to someone's home for dinner could expect either roast beef or turkey for the main course; if any alcoholic beverage was offered with the meal, it would probably be beer. But time brings changes, and Americans have become increasingly sophisticated in the matter of food and drink. Instead of a hackneyed, oft-repeated main course, guests are offered *coq au vin rouge* (chicken in red wine), *canard aux olives* (duck with olives), or *boeuf Bourguignonne* (beef in red wine). On the majority of occasions, the host will offer wine to his guests. Not infrequently, the host or hostess will remark that they first discovered the wine at a small country inn while touring France, Italy, or Spain, and how much they enjoyed it.

That is how the pattern began, how it continued and developed. First, Americans toured Europe and drank the local wine and ate the local cuisine. Once home, they sought out cook books with foreign recipes, and searched the liquor stores for their favorite wines. Foreign dishes and wines were served to their guests, and thus more and more people were exposed to European cooking and wines. Americans have responded with enthusiasm, as evidenced by the rapidly mounting sales of wines, and cook books with foreign recipes.

What is wine, and what purpose does it serve? It is a completely natural beverage, being made from the juice of crushed grapes. There are hundreds of different kinds of grapes, grown in different countries, under many varied climatic conditions, and picked and processed by thousands of vintners; it is this variation in the end product that makes wines so fascinating, because there are literally thousands of different types. Wine originated many thousands of years ago, perhaps back in prehistoric times. In any event, the Bible speaks of it as a well-loved, familiar part of daily life. Water was often unsafe to drink, and wine was always pure, so it was only natural for wine to supplant water as a regular beverage. Over and above the safety factor of wine as opposed to water, was the fact that wine offered a special and rather delicious taste. In most parts of the world today the danger of contaminated water has decreased, and indeed has largely disappeared, but the popularity of wine continues unabated, and has increased steadily. Without doubt, it is the taste of wine that accounts for its public acceptance.

The remarkable thing about wine is that it actually improves the taste of food, and a co-relationship has been built up between food and wine over more than a thousand years. A delicious, skillful creation of a talented chef may have a superb taste; a fine bottle of wine may also, in its own way, have a superb taste. Peculiarly enough, the two together create a sort of harmony of flavors that makes both the dish and the wine taste even better than either does alone. Why this should be so is difficult to explain, but the "marriage" of tastes works to the advantage of both the food and wine. Furthermore, a mediocre dish may often be raised to a remarkably fine-tasting preparation by the addition of wine, for just as a glass of wine improves the taste of food, so does wine used in cooking improve the dish.

Many people are hesitant about ordering wine, being fearful of ordering the wrong wine with the wrong food. So much has been written about wine-drinking, and about the lore of wine, that many people assume that it is a difficult, perhaps esoteric science, which can be learned only after many years of apprenticeship. This is far from accurate, and anyone can become knowledgeable about the correct wines with the correct foods in a matter of minutes. Needless to say, becoming an authority on the subject of wines requires years of practice and a sensitive palate. But enjoying wines—that is something completely different. That comes almost immediately.

Inasmuch as wines have been drunk with meals for thousands of years, it is only natural that certain opinions have developed about what wines are most suited with certain foods. First, sweet dessert wines have been excluded from the category of table wines, because these are cloying and rich, and would spoil the taste of the food (this excludes port, Madeira, Marsala, and other sweet wines), although these wines may be used in cooking. The only wines to be served with food are the non-sweet type; the word "dry" is often used to describe these unsweetened wines, because they leave a sort of "dry" taste in the mouth and because they are low in sugar. At first taste, unaccompanied by food, a dry wine may seem a trifle displeasing to the palate; when taken with food, its dry quality will soon be found to enhance the natural taste of the particular food.

Over the years, a few basic principles have evolved, first and foremost of which is this simple basic premise: white wines with fish, red wines with meat. That simple fact is easily remembered, because the colors roughly match; most fish dishes are whitish, and most meats are red, and so are the wines that best accompany them. No one need be an absolute conformist, and if you wish to drink a white wine with red meat, that is your privilege. But first, everyone should at least try the combinations suggested by the mass of opinion accumulated by literally millions of wine-drinkers over thousands of years.

That simple rule of white wines with fish and red wines with meat can be readily applied, but a few exceptions come to mind. Certain meats are classifiable as white meats (when cooked), such as veal and pork; with these "white" meats, you could enjoy equally a red or a white wine. The same rule applies to chicken, with which either white or red wine is suitable. With duck or goose, however, a red wine is far better than a white. Also, cheese is always better with a red wine than with a white, and the same applies to spaghetti or *pasta* dishes, except when the *pasta* is served with a fish sauce, in which case a white wine would be more suitable.

There has been a great deal of discussion about "vintage" wines. A vintage wine is the product of a particular year, and is referred to, for example, as the vintage of 1959. Americans are inclined to place unwarranted emphasis upon vintages; they often forget that even in good years, some bad wine is produced. On the other side of the coin, some good wine is produced even in years of a poor vintage.

Wines should be served at appropriate temperatures. White wines are always chilled; about three (or more) hours in a refrigerator will be sufficient. This is true except for champagne: because of its thick bottle, champagne requires almost six hours. If you are fortunate enough to own a wine bucket, fill it with plenty of ice cubes and cold water and revolve the wine bottle in it a few times; the intense cold will chill it in a matter of twenty to thirty minutes. White wines need not be opened until you are ready to serve them.

Red wines are different. First, they are served at what is called "room temperature"; however, the room temperature is that of a European home, where even today, central heating is not common. European room temperature means about 60–65°, not the 70° or more of American steam-heated homes. Red wines may be brought to correct temperature (if your home is warmer) by placing them briefly in the refrigerator (not more than twenty minutes), which will cool them slightly. Although white wines do not have to be opened in advance, red wines are best when the cork is removed about two hours before serving time. This allows the wines to "breathe," that is, to take in air. Because red wines have a heavier body than white wines, it is desirable that a little air be allowed to enter the freshly opened bottle, resulting in an improved taste. However, the earlier opening of red wines is not essential, but it does give additional quality.

Wine glasses should, wherever possible, be made of thin clear glass; thick glass is unpleasant to use and is not very esthetic. In the not very distant past, there were special wine glasses for every different wine, but in these days of limited domestic help and lack of storage space, only two principal types of glasses for wine remain. The red-wine glass is a fairly large, bowl-shaped glass (about the size and shape of a small orange) on a thin stem; the white-wine glass is a smaller version, about half the size of the red-wine glass. If you wish, only one type of wine glass need be used, but this should be the red-wine glass, which can also be used for white wines. On the other hand, the white-wine glass would be too small for the red wine, which needs room to "breathe." White-wine glasses should be half-filled, but red-wine glasses should not be filled more than one-third.

If there is any left-over wine, it may keep for a day or so, providing the bottle is promptly corked and placed in the refrigerator. Left-over red wine should, of course, be removed from the refrigerator the following day about two hours before serving time, to allow it to come to "room temperature." It is rare for an opened bottle of wine to keep for more than a day; after that, it will turn sour, and should not be drunk, or used in cooking. Don't open too much wine; the average bottle holds enough to serve 6-8 people with one glass each, but most people drink about two glasses with a meal. For a dinner party of 6-8 people, allow two bottles of wine.

TABLE WINES OF FOREIGN LANDS

Wines are produced on every continent of the world, although Asia accounts for the least. Wine production on a large scale is carried on, however, in Europe, Africa, North and South America, and Australia. Europe was and still is the center of the wine trade, and France produces the greatest variety of any country in the world. It is to France that everyone turns for any comparisons on production, types, tastes, and kinds of wine.

France

The two principal wine regions of France are Bordeaux and Burgundy. Considering Bordeaux first, this region lies in the southwestern part of the country, adjacent to the Atlantic Ocean, in a rather dreary, flat region. Bordeaux produces many of the finest wines in the world, and in addition a fair proportion of rather mediocre tables wines, called *vin ordinaire* in France. The red wines of Bordeaux vary from a pale red to a very deep shade, and from a light body to a medium-heavy body. The white wines are somewhat less distinguished, except for a group of dessert wines, sweet and rich, the Sauternes. The table white wines are pleasant, but not very important. The Bordeaux region is subdivided into five principal districts—Pomerol, Médoc, Saint-Emilion, Graves, and Sauternes. In the year 1855, the wines of two of these districts—Médoc and Sauternes—were classified by the *Syndicat des Courtiers*, the Society of Wine Brokers. They found four wines to be outstanding—Château Lafite-Rothschild, Margaux, Latour, and Haut-Brion. They omitted from their list the highly regarded wine of Mouton-Rothschild, placing it at the head of the second category. The canny wine brokers of 1855 have been proven substantially correct, because for more than a century these five wines have been excellent wines (with the exception of some poor years), and should have been included in the first rank, and the fact have commanded the highest prices. Mouton-Rothschild that even today it often is in the greatest demand of any of the five helps to prove the point. However, only millionaires could afford to drink these wines regularly; their price is inevitably high. Other excellent and less expensive wines of Bordeaux that have come to the fore include Leoville-Poyferre, Rauzan-Gassies, Rausan-Segla, Gruaud-Larose, Pichon-Longueville, Palmer, Calon-Segur, Talbot, Beychevelle, Pontet-Canet, Lynch-Bages, and Mouton-d'Armailhacq.

In Bordeaux, grapes are grown on large tracts of land popularly called châteaux, because originally the lord of the region lived in a large mansion, or château. The name of the château—such as Château Margaux, for example— is a complete assurance that all of the wine sold under that label has been cultivated, harvested, processed, and bottled by the same firm. This is not true in Burgundy, where large châteaux are unknown. For one thing, a much smaller amount of land is involved. Furthermore, under the French law of inheritance, children are entitled to inherit equal shares in the property of their father. Therefore, when the owner of a vineyard dies, if he has three children, each inherits a one-third interest in the vineyard, and when the original owner's grandsons ultimately inherit their parents' shares there will often be still further division. This is not the situation in Bordeaux, where large vineyards are owned by powerful syndicates with a perpetual, corporate-type existence.

Burgundy, France's other great wine region, lies southeast of Paris and stretches from Dijon south to Lyons. In this comparatively small area, several of the world's great red wines (and at least one truly great white wine) are produced. The grapes grow in a narrow strip, less than a mile wide and extending for only 36 miles, and the countryside consists of a range of gentle slopes, which furnished this smiling land with its secondary name, the Cote d'Or, or Slopes of Gold. The average altitude of the better vineyards is about 800 feet; wine grapes grown on lower or higher altitudes are quite inferior.

Frenchmen, more than almost any other nationality, are extremely individualistic, and like to do things in their own particular way. For this reason, even though a vineyard name appears on a bottle of Burgundy, if several different firms processed the wine it is often (in fact usually) different from another similarly named bottle, even though both bear the same name. In some extreme cases, where there were a dozen different owners of the same vineyard, there were twelve quite different products. Some of the great red wines produced in Burgundy include Chambertin, Musigny, Clos Vougeot, Romanee-Conti, Echezaux, Nuits-St.-Georges, Pommard, and Volnay. The great white wine of Burgundy, perhaps the finest in the world, is Montrachet, a wine of great delicacy, flavor, and aroma.

One wine deserves some special mention, Beaujolais. It is produced just north of the city of Lyons, in the direction of Macon. The wine is made chiefly from the Gamay grape, one known for its high production, but not for its quality. The resulting wine is comparatively low in price, has a fruity taste, and is quite delicious to drink, but lacks subtlety. Of all red wines, it is perhaps one of the best for those who wish to become acquainted with wines at moderate cost. Also noteworthy is Chablis, a rather good white wine produced about eighty miles to the northwest of Dijon.

Another important wine region of France is the Rhone Valley, extending southward from Lyons to Avignon, over 1,000 miles. Both red and white wines are produced here, but the reds are better known. Like the Beaujolais, they have a pleasing quality, but are seldom important and are lower in price than most wines of Bordeaux and Burgundy. The three great names here are Hermitage, Cote-Rotie, and Chateauneuf-du-Pape.

There are other wines produced all over France—for example, the light wines of the Loire Valley, the fruity wines of Alsace, and especially the most publicized wine in the world—champagne. Champagne is a white wine made from both black and white grapes, which are so treated and processed as to result in a pale gold wine, sparkling and delightful. Many people say that champagne may be drunk with fish, meat, or dessert. But I think that champagne is not very good with meat, and I do not recommend it. Champagnes are prepared in five principal types, for various tastes and markets. *Brut* contains ½ to 1% of sugar; *Extra Dry*, or *Extra Sec*, contains from 1 to 2%; *Sec*, or *Dry*, has from 3 to 6%; *Demi-Sec* contains from 7 to 10%, and *Doux* has 10 to 15%.

Germany

German wines are not in the same class with those of France for sheer variety, but German wines include some of the finest and most expensive in the world. Germany, however, has no good red wine, in fact not even a passable one; its fame rests exclusively with its white wines. The German white wines tend to have a flowery bouquet, a low alcoholic content, and a most attractive light gold color, with a somewhat greenish undertone.

The wine region of Germany is located in the western part of the country, a comparatively short distance to the east of the French province of Alsace. It is quite far north, and this factor hinders large-scale wine production, but often results in some extraordinarily fine vintages. The most important wines are produced in two river valleys— the Rhine and the Moselle.

Because this region is well to the north, away from the hot sunshine of the south, the grapes often do not have sufficient sunshine to permit them to mature properly. For this reason, while the ordinary harvest time in France is late September or early October, in Germany it does not come until the middle of October, and this brings with it the ever-present danger of sudden frost. There have even been years when German wines were not harvested until November.

Italy

Italy is one of the largest producers of wine in the world, and also probably the greatest consumer. Unlike France and Germany, which have their respective wine districts, Italy has vineyards that extend from one end of the country to another; there is no province, village, or farm without its wines, for the climate is such that grapes can be grown anywhere in that sunny country. Because the weather is fairly consistent (unlike that of France and

Germany), the wine crop never fails completely, but great vintages or great wines are unlikely. Italian white wines are pleasant to drink, and almost everyone likes them, but they cannot begin to compare with the finest products of France and Germany. Some of the best white wines of Italy are (not in any order of merit) Soave, white Chianti, Verdicchio, Frascati, Orvieto, and Capri.

The red wines are far better; most of them are what is called "drinkable," meaning they need not be slowly sipped, but can be drunk in gulps. Most Italian red wines lack the finesse of their French equivalent, but the average Italian does not fuss with wines the way a Frenchman does; the wines are there to drink and enjoy—and forget about vintages, and balance, and all of that nonsense. The most interesting red wines include Barolo, Barbaresco, Barbera, Gattinara, Grignolino, Sassella, Bardolino, Valpolicella, and, of course, Chianti. A word about this extremely popular wine: ordinary Chianti comes to the market in a straw-covered *fiasco*, which is necessary because the bottle has a rounded bottom and could not otherwise be placed upon the table. There is also an aged type called Chianti Classico, which reaches the market in regular bottles, and is far better.

Spain

Spain produces both red and white table wines, none of which are great, but are pleasant to drink. The two leading types are Rioja and Valdepenas. Nearby, in Portugal, a whole group of table wines are produced, including red, white, and *rosé* (pink). Some of the better-known Portuguese wines include Colares, Dao, and Grandjo. An interesting novelty is made in this country, *vinho verde*, green wine, a term that refers to the youth of the wine, not to its color. They are low in alcohol, slightly sparkling, and have a pleasant bouquet; the whites are far better than the reds.

Switzerland

The Swiss produce some light, rather unimportant table wines, but they do not travel well because of their low alcoholic content, and tend to lose their taste when they reach the United States. Although wine is produced all over Switzerland, the best comes from three regions—Vaud, Valais, and Neuchâtel.

North and South Africa

North Africa has a great deal of wine production in Algeria, Morocco, and Tunis. Many of these wines are shipped to France in bulk, so that their comparatively high alcoholic strength may be blended with weak Gallic products in poor years. In South Africa the vineyards extend some 160 miles to the east of Cape Town. The white wines of South Africa are undistinguished; the reds are far more interesting.

South America

Almost all the countries of South America (except Colombia and Venezuela) engage in some form of wine production, but Argentina and Chile are foremost in this field. In Argentina, much of the better wine is produced around Mendoza; almost all types of European wines are imitated here, some with more success than others. Probably the best wines of South America are made in Chile; although Argentina actually produces three times as much, Chile's product is generally superior.

TABLE WINES OF THE UNITED STATES

The wines of the United States have frequently been maligned, often by those who draw hasty conclusions. There is good wine being produced in this country, and the amount of it seems to be growing steadily.

But let's begin at the very beginning, usually a good starting place. Every schoolchild knows the story of the first exploration of the continent of North America by Leif the Lucky and his band of Vikings, who reached the continent in open boats, about the year 1000. Leif found so many wild grapes growing that he named the newly discovered region Vineland. The American Indians ate the grapes, but did not know the process of wine-making. It was Europeans who brought the techniques to the region. Afterward, when the settlers pushed westward to what is now California, wine-making truly began. There is considerable folklore, virtually completely unsupported by facts, that Father Junípero Serra planted the first vines at the mission in San Diego, possibly after 1769. True or not, it is almost certainly a fact that the Franciscan order built twenty-one mission houses and grew grapes for wine at the majority of them. All of these plantings were made with vines brought from Europe, of the type called *vitis vinifera*; the local vines were largely disregarded.

The first serious plantings on a more sophisticated basis were made by a Frenchman named Vignes, an appropriate name indeed, around 1830; he used cuttings brought from Bordeaux. About twenty years later, a Hungarian nobleman, bearing the complex name of Agoston Haraszthy, came to California. He, too, experienced fair success, also using European vines. In 1861, after considerable publicity, he became well known enough for the governor of California to call him in as an expert on wine production. Haraszthy was asked to go to Europe and bring back large numbers of vines for planting in the California area. He returned with over 100,000 cuttings from some 250 different grape varieties. Unfortunately, the Hungarian recommended the greatest possible diversification of wine production, including white, red, rosé, sweet dessert wines, and sparkling wines. In this way, California began to imitate the wines of every important wine region of the world. In any event, serious professional wine-making in California dates back to this time, a little more than a century ago. It was during the 1880s that the first dozen important wineries were founded.

The origin of wine-making in the eastern part of the country was somewhat different. The first attempts to grow European vines were a failure from the start, chiefly because the climate was unsuitable. When the eastern wine-makers turned to native vines they were far more successful. Using vines such as the Delaware, Elvira, and Catawba (and subsequently hybrid vines), they produced some interesting but different wines for which they had no basis of comparison. Eventually, certain standards were developed for eastern wines, which had a distinctive taste and unusual quality. As time passed, the New York vineyards have tended to concentrate almost exclusively upon white wines, leaving the reds to California.

During the period from 1880 to 1920, the wineries of California made determined efforts to improve their products and market them with dignity. When Prohibition came, many vineyards were forced by circumstances to switch to producing sacramental wines and marketing table grapes and raisins. In 1933, when Prohibition ended, they turned to wine-making once again. About ten years later, the product had returned to pre-Prohibition standards.

Now, let's turn to the actual wines themselves. For the sake of discussion, there are really only two areas—California, and the other regions of the country. About 90 percent of American wines come from California. The remaining 10 percent is divided among the Finger Lakes region of upper New York State, northern Ohio, and some small areas of New Jersey, Virginia, the Carolinas, Georgia, Michigan, Tennessee, and Missouri. We will consider California wines first.

The soil and climate of this enormous state are so variable that almost any conceivable wine growing area of the world can be duplicated. There are cool valleys, dry or moist plains, deserts, sloping hills, and rolling country-side; it has been found that every European grape type, every *vitis vinifera*, will grow *somewhere* in California.

California wines are readily divided into three chief categories, for the purpose of discussion and explanation: they are the European generic type, the grape varietal, and the region in which the vineyard is located. If this sounds a trifle confusing at first, it is far from that, with a little in the way of illustration.

The phrase *European generic type* refers to the European name of the wine which the California vintner is attempting to imitate. For example, Burgundy is a well-recognized wine region of France, with hundreds of different wines. However, any wine produced in that region may be called a Burgundy wine, and is generally characterized by a hearty, rich quality, often called "masculine," as opposed to other, softer wines which may be designated as "feminine" in nature. Thus, any California wine producer may label as Burgundy any red wine he produces, although the resemblance may not be great.

Now, turning to the second classification of California wines, we find grape varietals. This rather elaborate term merely refers to the actual name of the vines producing the grapes, such as Pinot Noir, Chardonnay, and so forth. It can be said that the best vintners are tending to bottle their products under the name of the grape varietal, or vine, rather than using the old European descriptive term, discussed above.

Lastly, California wines may be classified according to the district in which the grapes are grown. By their nature, the very best grapes apparently grow best in comparatively cool climates, and therefore the finest regions are those of the northern coastal regions of California. These include Sonoma, Napa, Livermore, Santa Clara, and Santa Cruz. When the wines are called by their district name, it means that the wine has been prepared from grapes that have been grown and fermented in the area specified to the extent of at least 75 percent. This obviously allows for

25 percent of wine from other, less desirable wine districts. It should also be mentioned that other counties of California produce very good wine, including Mendocino, San Benito, Solano, and Cucamonga.

Returning once again to the classification of grape varietals, that is, the name of the vine used in the making of the particular wine, it has been found that the most successful white wines are being made with the Traminer and Sylvaner grapes, which have tended to produce a drier wine, with a higher alcoholic content than in Germany. The Pinot Blanc and the Chardonnay grapes produce a reasonably good type of Chablis. In California, they regularly market a sweet and also a dry type of Sauterne (they leave off the final s from the French word Sauternes). The sweet Sauterne is made chiefly from the sweet Semillon; the dry Sauterne is sold under the label of the grape type Sauvignon Blanc and Semillon.

California rosé wines are becoming increasingly popular with the American public; the better pink wine is made from the Grenache Rosé grape, and the more routine produce from the Gamay.

Now, turning to red wines, when the California vintners wish to imitate France's claret (from the Bordeaux region), the Cabernet Sauvignon grape is used. It produces a rather good wine, although it bears only a modest degree of resemblance to the French original. However, we take a big step forward with the Pinot Noir, used to make the California version of Burgundy. As a rule, a bottle of California's Pinot Noir, so labeled, is likely to be a very acceptable bottle of red wine. Other red wine grapes used on a large scale are Gamay, Gamay Beaujolais, Barbera, Zinfandel, and Grignolino. These grapes tend to result in wines that are fruity and pleasant, easy to drink, somewhat like France's Beaujolais, or Italy's Chianti.

As a matter of our opinion, we submit the following very personal list which includes some of the better wines of California:

CALIFORNIA RED WINES
Cabernet-Sauvignon
(like red Bordeaux wines)

Almáden Cabernet Sauvignon
Beaulieu Vineyard Cabernet Sauvignon
Gemello Cabernet
Inglenook Cabernet Sauvignon
Charles Krug Cabernet Sauvignon
Louis Martini Cabernet Sauvignon
Souverain Cellars Cabernet Sauvignon

Pinot Noir
(like red Burgundy)

Almáden Pinot Noir
Beaulieu Pinot Noir
Buena Vista Pinot Noir
Inglenook Pinot Noir
Louis Martini Pinot Noir
Paul Masson Pinot Noir
Martin Ray Pinot Noir

Other Red Wines
(similar to European carafe wines)

Buena Vista Zinfandel
Cresta Blanca Chianti Reserve
Cucamonga Winery Barbera
Louis Martini Barbera and Zinfandel
Digardi Mountain Gamay
Paul Masson Gamay Beaujolais
San Martin Zinfandel

CALIFORNIA WHITE WINES
Pinot Blanc and Pinot Chardonnay
(similar to a white Burgundy)

Almáden Pinot Blanc
Beaulieu Vineyard Pinot Chardonnay
Charles Krug White Pinot
Inglenook Pinot Chardonnay

Novitiate of Los Gatos Pinot Blanc
Weibel Pinot Chardonnay
Wente Pinot Blanc
Wente Pinot Chardonnay

Sauvignon Blanc and Semillon
(similar to a dry Bordeaux white wine)

Almáden Dry Semillon
Concannon Dry Semillon
Cresta Blanca Premier Semillon
Louis Martini Dry Semillon
Paul Masson Semillon

Sweet Semillon and Chenin Blanc
(similar to sweet Sauternes)

Beaulieu Vineyard Chateau Beaulieu
Concannon Sweet Semillon
Charles Krug Chenin Blanc
Wente Sweet Semillon

Riesling, Traminer, Sylvaner
(like Rhine or Alsatian wines)

Almáden Johannisberg Riesling
Beaulieu Vineyard Johannisberg Riesling
Buena Vista Sylvaner
Buena Vista Traminer
Inglenook Riesling
Louis Martini Johannisberg Riesling
Souverain Cellars Sylvaner

Grenache and Gamay Rosé
(similar to European rosé wines)

Almáden Grenache Rosé
Beaulieu Grenache Rosé
Cresta Blanca Reserve Rosé
Louis Martini Gamay Rosé
Mayacamas Vineyards Gamay Rosé
Souverain Cellars Grenache Rosé

As previously mentioned, about 90 percent of American wines come from California. New York State contributes somewhere in the neighborhood of 7 or 8 percent of the remainder of American wines, but included among them are some very worthwhile products.

It should be understood, for this is most important, that the New York wines are made from a totally different variety of grape than those of California (with the exception of some small plantings to be discussed later). The grapes grown in Europe and subsequently in California are called *vitis vinifera;* these had a certain smooth and even taste. The native American grape, found by the first settlers, are of a variety called *vitis labrusca.* When the earliest wine growers tasted their first bottlings, they were disconcerted by the strange and somewhat "wild" taste of their wine. Sometimes the flavor is described as raw, but the most frequently used term is "foxy." Dictionaries tend to fumble when defining this word, but it generally means a very "grapy" taste, certainly more than a European wine normally has. Perhaps this taste is caused by the greater amount of acid produced by *labrusca* grapes, as compared with the *vinifera* type.

There can be no doubt, however, that New York wines are quite different from those produced in California, and Europe. Red wines are not too successful when produced in the Empire State, but the white wines do have their points, if one is willing to accept wines which are unlike those produced by the *vinifera* grape. After centuries of experimentation, only the riesling grape, of all European grape types, is grown in this part of the country, although of course, there are numerous hybrids. New York wines are sold under two classifications: the generic names which imitate European wine names such as New York State Chablis, and, second, under the name of the grape chiefly used in making the wine such as Niagara, Diana, and so forth.

Previously, it was mentioned that New York wines of the *labrusca* type are comparatively high in acid content, and to counterbalance this sugar is generally added. (In California, there is enough hot sunshine to produce natural sugar in the grapes, but this seldom occurs in New York.)

It should be remembered, however, that adding sugar doesn't necessarily mean that a sweet wine will result, bcause the sugar is added primarily to induce fermentation of the grapes.

New York State champagne is quite different from the still white wines. When the finished product is ready to drink, it has none of the "foxy" or wild quality associated with ordinary still white wines. In France and California, most champagne producers use Pinot Noir and Chardonnay grapes, but inasmuch as these will not grow satisfactorily in the east, New York champagne producers use Delaware and Catawba grapes, and sometimes several of the hybrid grapes. The result is surprisingly satisfactory, all things considered. The two leading brands are Great Western and Fournier Blanc de Blanc, both of which are fermented in the bottle, in the French manner. If the label says it's Champagne-Style, that means it is produced in large vats by the "bulk" process rather than individually in each bottle.

To sum up: New York State wines sold as Chablis or Sauternes, and so forth, are not usually of the best quality, and have little in common with the names furnished to them. However, many of the premium wines produced in New York State, and sold under the name of the grape used such as Elvira, Niagara, Delaware, and others, are likely to be quite good.

Some interesting experiments have been conducted in New York, in the attempt once again to grow the European *vinifera* type of grape, particularly in the vicinity of Hammondsport. There is hope that in the years to come New York State will also find a way in which to grow successfully many European types of grapes. But, of course, only time will tell if this can be accomplished in large quantities and on a commercial basis.

YOUR OWN WINE CELLAR

Nothing is pleasanter for wine enjoyment than devoting a small place in your home to wines. Of course, it is always possible to buy a bottle of wine as required, but wines are better when allowed a few days of rest, so that they may settle. Of course, a cellar in a private house is an ideal place for this, but it is not essential. Any cool dark place, free from drafts, away from cooking odors, and without extremes of heat and cold (no steam pipes, air-conditioning, etc.) will do. It may be a closet or any other spare space. The ideal temperature is 55°, but slightly higher or lower is permissible if there are no wide fluctuations. If there is danger of extreme cold or heat, the storage space should be lined with insulating material, which can be purchased at almost any hardware store. The wine bottles must, of course, be stored on their sides, so that the wine is actually in contact with the corks; otherwise the corks will dry out and the wine spoil. Good department stores sell wine racks made of wood or metal, with compartments for each individual bottle, should you wish to spend the money for this pleasant luxury.

Many wines are now available in half bottles; this is an ideal way of tasting, and of essaying your likes and dislikes at comparatively moderate cost. Some wine and liquor stores will allow you to buy a case of assorted half bottles (at cash prices), and this practice can be recommended to those who have a high degree of curiosity about the relative tastes and flavors of different wines. After sampling a large group, it should be fairly easy in the future to select several favorites.

Another good way to begin is by purchasing a small basic wine cellar, consisting of say, a half-dozen or more bottles, and costing about $20 to $25. Naturally, any such list would be a matter of personal choice, but the following should act as a guide.

Red Wines:

1 Bordeaux (Gruard-Larose, Pontet-Canet, Leoville-Poyferre)
1 Burgundy (Volnay, Nuits-St. Georges, Chambertin)
1 Italian (Chianti, Valpolicella, Bardolino)
1 American (Pinot Noir, Cabernet-Sauvignon)

White Wines:

1 French (Pouilly-Fuissé, Pouilly-Fumé)
1 Italian (Verdicchio, Orvieto, Soave)
1 German (Piesporter, Johannisberger)
1 American (Pinot Blanc, Sauvignon Blanc)

Now, what about wine in cooking? As previously mentioned, wines enhance the flavor of foods, bringing out un-
realized subtleties of taste. For thousands of years, wine has
been used as a cooking ingredient all over Europe, and the
quality of European culinary art is well recognized the
world over. In cookery, all of the rules about white wines
with fish and red wines with meat, and about not using
sweet wines, may be disregarded, because the cooking
process changes all of that. Thus, many recipes in this
book call for a white wine to be used with meat, or a red
wine with a fish dish; exceptions for these cooking pro-
cedures do not cancel out or nullify what has been previously stated about drinking wines. Furthermore, no
mother need feel the slightest qualms about feeding her
children any dish made with wine; if the dish is cooked,
the heat will evaporate all of the alcohol in the wine,
making it perfectly suitable for serving even very young
children.

As we go through life, we find that few pleasures remain
as consistently rewarding as good food and good wine.
Each alone is very worthwhile; the two together are often
superb.

SHRIMP SOUFFLÉ

1 cup water
1 cup dry white wine
2 teaspoons salt
1 onion
1 pound raw shrimp,
   shelled and deveined
3 tablespoons butter

3 tablespoons flour
1/2 cup heavy cream
1/2 teaspoon dry mustard
1/8 teaspoon cayenne
   pepper
4 egg yolks
4 egg whites

Combine the water, 1/2 cup wine, 1 teaspoon salt, and the onion in a saucepan; bring to a boil. Add the shrimp, reduce heat, and cook over low heat 5 minutes. Drain. Strain the stock, reserving 1/4 cup. Chop shrimp coarsely.

Melt the butter in a saucepan and stir in the flour. Gradually mix in the reserved stock, the remaining wine, and the cream, stirring steadily to the boiling point. Blend in the mustard, remaining salt, and the cayenne pepper; cook over low heat 5 minutes. Beat the egg yolks in a bowl; gradually mix in the hot sauce, stirring constantly to prevent curdling. Stir in the shrimp. Cool 10 minutes.

Beat the egg whites until stiff but not dry; fold into the shrimp mixture gently. Turn into a buttered 1 1/2-quart soufflé dish; bake in a preheated 375° oven 35 minutes, or until browned and set. Serve immediately.

Serve with a California or New York white wine, a dry white Burgundy, a dry white German wine, or a Loire Valley wine like Pouilly-Fumé.

Serves 4-6

SPICED SHRIMP

2 cups water
2 cups dry white wine
2 teaspoons salt
1/4 teaspoon Tabasco
2 cloves
3 allspice
6 peppercorns

2 bay leaves
2 cloves garlic, minced
1 cup chopped celery
   and leaves
6 sprigs parsley
2 pounds raw shrimp,
   shelled and deveined

Combine and bring to a boil all the ingredients but the shrimp. Add the shrimp, bring to a boil again, and cook over low heat 6 minutes. Cool the shrimp in the liquid, then chill at least 4 hours. Drain thoroughly. Pierce shrimp with cocktail picks or toothpicks for hors d'oeuvres, or serve as a first course.

Serves 6-8 as a first course.

Serve with a Loire wine like Pouilly-Fumé, a dry German white wine, a white Burgundy, or a dry white American wine.

SHRIMP COCKTAIL WITH SHERRY SAUCE

1 pound cooked shrimp, cleaned	1/2 cup chili sauce
1 cup diced cucumbers	1/4 cup dry sherry
1/4 cup mayonnaise	1 teaspoon prepared horseradish

Dice the shrimp and toss with the cucumbers. Mix together the mayonnaise, chili sauce, sherry, and horseradish. Toss with the shrimp. Chill 1 hour before serving.

Serve with a dry California or New York white wine, dry German white wine, a Loire Valley wine like Pouilly-Fumé or Vouvray; or if you wish, with a *rosé*.

Serves 4-6

SHRIMP IN PAPERS

1/4 pound Roquefort cheese	1 1/2 pounds uncooked shrimp, shelled and deveined
1/2 pound cream cheese	
3/4 cup dry white wine	6 slices lemon
1/2 cup chopped stuffed green olives	

Cream the Roquefort cheese and cream cheese until smooth; add the wine gradually, then the olives.

Cut 6 pieces of parchment paper or aluminum foil about 12 inches square; divide the cheese mixture among them and cover with several shrimp and a lemon slice. Bring two edges of the paper together and fold twice. Bring up other sides, and twist to make a secure closing. Bake in a 400° oven 30 minutes. Serve in the papers.

Note: Smaller versions make excellent hot hors d'oeuvres.

Serve with a dry American white wine, a dry German white wine, a white Burgundy, or any dry Italian white wine like Verdicchio.

Serves 6

SCALLOPS LUTETIA

1 1/2 pounds scallops	1 teaspoon salt
6 tablespoons butter	1/4 teaspoon white
1 1/2 cups sliced	pepper
mushrooms	3 egg yolks
1 cup heavy cream	
2 cups champagne, or	
dry white wine	

Wash and dry the scallops. If sea scallops are used, cut in half crosswise. Leave bay scallops whole.

Melt 3 tablespoons of the butter in a deep skillet; sauté the scallops for 3 minutes. Add the mushrooms, cream, wine, salt, and pepper. Cook over medium heat for 5 minutes. Remove the scallops and keep them warm. Cook the sauce over high heat until reduced to half.

Beat the egg yolks in a bowl. Gradually add the sauce, beating constantly to prevent curdling. Return the mixture to skillet with the scallops and the remaining butter. Reheat, but do not allow to boil. Taste for seasoning.

Serve with champagne, a dry American white wine, a dry white Burgundy, or a dry German white wine.

Serves 6-8

CRABMEAT LUCULLUS

2 pounds crab meat	1 1/2 teaspoons salt
4 tablespoons butter	Dash cayenne pepper
4 tablespoons flour	3/4 cup dry white wine
2 cups light cream	

Pick over the crab meat, discarding any cartilage.

Melt the butter in a saucepan. Blend in the flour until smooth. Add the cream, stirring constantly to the boiling point. Mix in the salt, cayenne, pepper, wine. Fold in the crab meat. Taste for seasoning.

Pour the mixture into a buttered 1 1/2-quart casserole. or into individual ovenproof dishes. Bake in a 400° oven 15 minutes.

Serve with a dry American white wine, a dry German white wine, a white Burgundy, or an Alsatian wine.

Serves 6-8

GRATIN D'HOMARD
(lobster au gratin)

4 1 1/4-pound lobsters or	2 tablespoons flour
8 African lobster tails	1 teaspoon salt
1/4 pound (1 stick) butter	1/8 teaspoon white pepper
1/4 pound mushrooms,	1 cup heavy cream
sliced	1/2 cup grated Gruyère or
3/4 cup dry white wine	Swiss cheese

Cook the lobster or tails in boiling salted water for 15 minutes. Drain and cool. Remove lobster meat; slice bodies and dice claws; or slice tail.

Melt 6 tablespoons butter in a skillet; sauté the lobster 5 minutes. Add the mushrooms, and sauté 2 minutes. Mix in the wine; cover, and cook over low heat 5 minutes. Mix the flour, salt, and pepper with the cream; add to the lobster, stirring constantly to the boiling point. Turn into a shallow baking dish or individual dishes. Sprinkle with cheese and dot with remaining butter. Bake in a 425° oven 10 minutes, or until delicately browned.

Serve with a dry American white wine, a white Burgundy, a champagne, a Loire Valley wine like Pouilly-Fumé, or a dry white Bordeaux.

Serves 4-8

OYSTERS WITH SEAFOOD SAUCE

1/2 pound raw shrimp,	1/8 teaspoon cinnamon
shelled and deveined	36 oysters on the half-shell
1/4 pound crab meat	1/2 cup grated Parmesan
1/2 cup dry white wine	cheese
1 cup chili sauce	

Chop the shrimp very fine; combine in a saucepan with the crab meat, wine, chili sauce, and cinnamon. Cover, and cook over low heat 20 minutes. Taste for seasoning.

Arrange the oysters on a baking pan, and spoon the sauce over them. Sprinkle with the cheese. Bake in a 475° oven until cheese browns.

Serves 6-8

BAKED OYSTERS AND CRAB MEAT

24 oysters on the half-shell
1 cup dry white wine
6 tablespoons butter
2 tablespoons flour
1/2 cup heavy cream
3/4 teaspoon salt
Dash cayenne pepper

1/2 pound crab meat, flaked
4 tablespoons dry bread crumbs

Remove the oysters from the shells. Scrub and dry the shells.

Bring the wine to a boil; add the oysters and cook over low heat 1 minute. Drain the oysters and strain the wine.

Melt 4 tablespoons of the butter in a saucepan; blend in the flour. Add the wine and cream, stirring steadily to the boiling point. Stir in the salt and cayenne pepper; cook over low heat 5 minutes. Mix the crab meat with 1/2 cup of the sauce; taste for seasoning. Divide the mixture among the shells and place an oyster over each. Cover with the remaining sauce, sprinkle with the bread crumbs, and dot with the remaining butter. Arrange on a baking sheet, and bake in a 475° oven 5 minutes. Serve immediately.

Serve with a white American wine, a white Burgundy, an Alsatian wine like Traminer, or a dry German white wine.

Serves 4-6

ESCARGOTS À LA BOURGUIGNONNE
(snails in garlic butter)

36 snails
1/3 pound butter
4 tablespoons finely chopped shallots or onion

1 tablespoon minced garlic
3 tablespoons minced parsley

1 tablespoon salt
1/4 teaspoon freshly
    ground black pepper

3/4 cup dry white wine
1/4 cup dry bread crumbs

If fresh snails are not available, buy canned snails, which come with shells separate.

Cream the butter and blend with the shallots, garlic, parsley, salt, and pepper. Place a little of the mixture in each shell and press a snail into it. Fill shells with remaining butter, packing in firmly. Arrange, filled side up, in 6 snail pans or a baking dish. Pour a little wine over them and sprinkle with bread crumbs. Bake in 425° oven 10 minutes.

Serve with a white American wine, a dry German white wine, champagne, or a Loire Valley wine like Pouilly-Fumé.

Serves 6

HERENGS MARINÉS
(marinated herring)

6 fresh herring
4 cups thinly sliced onions
2 tablespoons pickling
    spice
1 tablespoon salt

2 bay leaves
2 cups dry white wine
1 cup white wine vinegar
1/3 cup salad oil

Split the herring and discard the heads and bones; cut herring in half crosswise. In a heatproof glass or earthenware skillet or casserole, spread a layer of onion slices on the bottom, with half the pickling spice, salt, and 1 bay leaf over them. Arrange alternate layers of herring and onion slices over this, ending with the onion slices and remaining pickling spice, salt, and other bay leaf. Add the wine and vinegar; cover, and cook over low heat 25 minutes. Cool, and pour the oil over the top. Re-cover and refrigerate 48 hours before serving. Keeps 4–6 weeks.

Note: If fresh herring is not available, then use salt herring. Soak in cold water 24 hours, changing the water a few times. Decrease salt in recipe to 1 teaspoon.

Serves 12-18

BOULETTES DE FROMAGE
(cheese balls)

8 ounces Camembert or Brie cheese	1 cup ground blanched almonds
1 cup dry white wine	Toasted blanched almonds
1/2 pound (2 sticks) butter, softened	

Carefully remove the rind of the cheese. Marinate the trimmed cheese in the wine 8 hours, turning it several times. Drain. Force the cheese through a food mill, or mash smooth. Beat in the butter. Chill 3 hours. Form teaspoons of the mixture into balls. Chill again, then roll in the ground almonds. Place a whole almond in each ball.

Makes about 60.

Serve with a dry red Bordeaux or Burgundy, a dry Italian red wine like Bardolino, or an American red wine.

DELICES D'EMMENTHAL
(fried cheese sticks)

4 tablespoons butter	3 egg yolks, beaten
1 1/3 cups sifted flour	1 egg
1/2 cup dry white wine	1/4 cup light cream
1 cup milk	1 tablespoon olive oil
3/4 teaspoon salt	3/4 cup dry bread crumbs
Dash cayenne pepper	1 cup vegetable oil
2 cups (1/2 pound) grated Swiss cheese	

Melt the butter in a saucepan; blend in 1/3 cup of the flour. Gradually add the wine and milk, stirring steadily to the boiling point. Stir in the salt and cayenne pepper; cook over low heat 10 minutes, stirring frequently. Remove from heat, and mix in the cheese until melted. Beat in the egg yolks.

Turn into a buttered oblong dish to a depth of 1 inch. Cover with foil or waxed paper and chill. Cut into strips about 3 inches long and 1/2 inch wide. Beat the whole egg with the cream and olive oil. Dip the sticks in the remaining flour, then in the egg mixture, and finally in the bread crumbs, coating them thoroughly.

Heat the vegetable oil in a skillet until it bubbles. Fry the sticks in it until browned on all sides. Drain. Don't crowd the pan, and keep oil very hot, or the sticks will melt.

Makes about 24.

Serve with an Alsatian wine like Riesling, an American white wine, a dry German white wine, or a dry red Bordeaux or Burgundy.

AUBERGINES À LA GRECQUE
(eggplant in oil)

1 medium eggplant	1/4 teaspoon thyme
2 teaspoons salt	4 peppercorns, crushed
1/2 cup olive oil	2 coriander seeds
3/4 cup dry white wine	1 1/2 cups peeled,
1 bay leaf	chopped tomatoes

Peel the eggplant, and cut as for french fried potatoes. Sprinkle with the salt, and let stand 30 minutes. Drain very well.

Heat the oil in a skillet; lightly brown the eggplant in it. Remove the eggplant. To the oil remaining in the skillet, add the wine, bay leaf, thyme, peppercorns, coriander seeds, and tomatoes. Bring to a boil, and cook over low heat 15 minutes. Return the eggplant to skillet. Cook over low heat 15 minutes. Taste for seasoning. Serve cold.

Serves 4

ARTICHOKES À LA GRECQUE

1 package frozen artichoke hearts	3 teaspoons lemon juice
12 very small white onions	1/2 cup dry white wine
	1 1/2 teaspoons salt
1 clove garlic, minced	1/4 teaspoon freshly ground black pepper
1/4 cup olive oil	1/4 cup water

Let the artichoke hearts thaw sufficiently to separate. In a saucepan, combine the remaining ingredients. Bring to a boil, and cook over low heat 25 minutes. Add the artichoke hearts. Cook 5 minutes. Taste for seasoning. Pour into a glass or pottery dish. Cool, then refrigerate until needed. Will keep about 2 weeks.

Serves 3-4

CAPPELLI DI FUNGHI RIPIENI
(stuffed mushroom caps)

2 pounds firm white mushrooms	1 teaspoon salt
4 tablespoons olive oil	1/4 teaspoon freshly ground black pepper
4 tablespoons butter	1 egg yolk, beaten
1 clove garlic, minced	1/2 cup dry bread crumbs
1 tablespoon flour	
1/2 cup dry white wine	

Wash and dry the mushrooms; remove the stems and chop them. Heat 1 tablespoon oil and 1 tablespoon butter in a skillet; sauté the mushrooms and garlic 2 minutes. Blend in the flour, and add the wine, salt, and pepper. Cook over medium heat 5 minutes, or until liquid is evaporated, stirring frequently. Cool 10 minutes, then mix in the egg yolk. Stuff the mushroom caps.

Pour the remaining oil into a shallow baking dish; arrange the mushrooms in it. Sprinkle with the bread crumbs and dot with the remaining butter. Bake in a 375° oven 15 minutes. Serve hot or cold.

Serve with champagne, or an American *rosé* wine.

Serves 4-6

OEUFS À LA BOURGUIGNONNE
(eggs in wine)

10 slices bacon, diced	1 cup beef broth
3 tablespoons butter	1 cup dry red wine
1/2 cup chopped onion	1 bay leaf
1 clove garlic, minced	1/8 teaspoon thyme
2 tablespoons flour	2 tablespoons minced parsley
1 1/4 teaspoons salt	8 eggs
1/4 teaspoon freshly ground black pepper	

Fry the bacon until crisp. Drain. Melt the butter in a saucepan; sauté the onion and garlic until lightly browned. Blend in the flour, salt, and pepper, then gradually add

the broth and wine, stirring steadily to the boiling point.
Add the bay leaf, thyme, and parsley; cook over low heat
20 minutes. Strain into a skillet. Bring to a boil again and
carefully poach the eggs in it, no more than 2 at a time.
Serve on sautéed or toasted French bread, with the sauce
over them, and the bacon sprinkled on top.

Serve with a dry red American wine, or a dry red Bordeaux or Burgundy, including a Beaujolais, a dry Italian
red wine like Bardolino.

Serves 4-8

UOVA ALLA CACCIATORA
(eggs, hunter's style)

1/4 pound chicken livers	1/4 teaspoon basil
4 tablespoons olive oil	1/4 cup peeled, chopped tomatoes
1/4 cup chopped onion	1/4 cup dry white wine
1 1/4 teaspoons salt	4 eggs
1/4 teaspoon freshly ground black pepper	4 slices buttered toast
	1 tablespoon parsley

Wash the livers, cut away any discolored spots. Cut in half.
Heat the oil in a skillet; sauté the chopped onions 5
minutes. Add the livers; sauté 5 minutes, mixing occasionally. Stir in the salt, pepper, basil, tomatoes, and wine.
Bring to a boil, and cook over low heat 5 minutes. Carefully break the eggs into the pan, cover, and cook until set,
about 3 minutes. Transfer each egg to a piece of toast and
cover with the sauce. Sprinkle with the parsley.

Serve with a dry red Bordeaux or Burgundy, a dry
Italian red wine like Barbera, or a dry California red wine.

Serves 2-4

EGGS AMANDINE

4 tablespoons butter	1/2 cup champagne or dry white wine
2 tablespoons grated onion	6 eggs
1/2 cup ground almonds	1/2 cup heavy cream
1/4 cup boiled ham, ground	1 teaspoon salt
	1/4 teaspoon freshly ground black pepper

Melt the butter in a skillet. Add the grated onion, almonds, and ham. Sauté for 5 minutes, stirring almost constantly. Add the champagne or white wine. Cook over low heat for 3 minutes.

Beat together the eggs, cream, salt, and pepper in a bowl. Pour over the almond mixture, and cook to desired consistency, stirring constantly. Do not overcook. Serve in patty shells or on toast squares.

Serve with a light red Bordeaux, Burgundy, a dry Italian red wine like Valpolicella, or a dry California red wine.

Serves 4-6

MOUSSE DE FOIE DE VOLAILLE
(chicken liver mousse)

1 pound chicken livers	1/4 cup heavy cream
3/8 pound (1 1/2 sticks) butter	3/4 teaspoon salt
1/4 cup chopped onion	1/4 teaspoon freshly ground black pepper
1/2 cup Madeira or sweet sherry	

Wash the livers, remove any discolored spots, and dry. Cut the livers in small pieces.

Melt 4 tablespoons butter in a skillet; sauté the livers and onion 5 minutes. Empty into a blender bowl or onto a board. Add the wine to the skillet; cook over high heat 5 minutes. Add to the livers. Purée in the blender, gradually adding the cream, salt, and pepper until a smooth paste is formed. Or chop very fine, gradually adding the cream and the seasoning, and force the mixture through a fine sieve. Taste for seasoning, and pack into a bowl or crock. Cover, and chill 4 hours. Serve in the crock, or unmold and serve with slices of French bread.

Makes about 2 cups.

Serve with a *rosé* wine, American or European.

KÄSEBRÖTCHEN
(wine-cheese toast)

6 slices stale bread	3/4 cup freshly grated Parmesan cheese
1 cup dry white wine	3 tablespoons butter
2 eggs, beaten	

Trim the crusts off the bread. Dip the slices one at a time in the wine. Beat the eggs and mix in the cheese. Dip the slices in the mixture, coating them well. Arrange on a well-buttered baking sheet and dot with the butter. Bake in a 375° oven 15 minutes, or until bread is browned, turning the slices once. Serve hot.

Serve with a white Swiss wine like Fendant, a dry German white wine, an Alsatian wine like Traminer, or a New York state white wine.

Serves 6

SWISS FONDUE

1 clove garlic	1/2 teaspoon salt
2 1/4 cups dry white wine	1/8 teaspoon white pepper
1 pound Gruyère or Swiss cheese, grated	1/8 teaspoon nutmeg
1 1/2 tablespoons potato flour	3 tablespoons kirsch (cherry liqueur)
	French bread cubes

A chafing dish is customarily used for making fondue. If you do not have one, use the bottom of a double boiler to hold the water, and an earthenware bowl for the fondue. Have enough hot water in the bottom part of the chafing dish or double boiler to barely touch the bowl. Light the burner of the chafing dish, or place double boiler over low heat.

Rub the chafing dish or bowl with the garlic and add 2 cups wine; place over the water. Heat the wine, then stir in the cheese until melted. Mix the potato flour with the remaining wine and add to the cheese mixture, stirring steadily. Let cook 3 minutes. Blend in the salt, pepper, nutmeg, and kirsch. Provide a fork for each guest with which to spear the cubes of French bread—the bread cubes should then be dipped in the fondue.

Serve with a white Swiss wine like Neuchâtel or Fendant, or an Alsatian wine like Traminer, a dry German white wine, or a dry American white wine.

Serves 4-6

SOUP

CIORBA DE CEAPA
(Rumanian onion soup)

3 tablespoons butter	2 tablespoons lemon juice
3 cups diced onion	1 teaspoon sugar
2 teaspoons sugar	1/4 teaspoon freshly
5 cups beef broth	ground black pepper
1 cup diced potatoes	1 cup heavy cream
1/4 teaspoon celery seed	2 tablespoons minced
1 cup dry white wine	parsley

Melt the butter in a saucepan; sauté the onions and sugar until browned. Add the broth, potato, and celery seed. Cover, bring to a boil, and cook over low heat 30 minutes. Purée in a blender, or force through a food mill.

Return to the saucepan and stir in the wine, lemon juice, sugar, and pepper. Bring to a boil, and cook over low heat 10 minutes. Gradually blend in the cream; heat, but do not let boil. Taste for seasoning, sprinkle with the parsley, and serve.

Serves 6-8

CREAMED ONION SOUP

4 tablespoons butter	1/4 teaspoon white
4 cups thinly sliced onion	pepper
1 1/2 tablespoons flour	2 egg yolks
4 cups chicken broth	1 cup heavy cream
2 cups dry white wine	Grated Gruyère or
1 teaspoon salt	Swiss cheese

Melt the butter in a saucepan; sauté the sliced onions over low heat until browned. Blend in the flour. Add the broth, wine, salt, and pepper, mixing steadily to the boiling point. Cover loosely, and cook over low heat 25 minutes.

Beat the egg yolks and cream in a bowl. Gardually add some of the hot soup, stirring steadily to prevent curdling.

Return to balance of soup. Taste for seasoning. Heat, stirring steadily, but do not let boil. Serve with a bowl of grated cheese.

Serves 6-8

CREAM OF MUSHROOM SOUP

1/2 cup dried mushrooms	2 cups milk
1/2 cup water	1 1/4 teaspoons salt
1 pound fresh mushrooms	1/4 teaspoon freshly
1/4 pound butter	ground black pepper
2 tablespoons flour	1/4 cup dry sherry
2 cups heavy cream	Minced parsley

Soak the dried mushrooms in the water for 2 hours. Drain, reserving the water, and chop.

Chop the stems of the fresh mushrooms. Melt the butter in a skillet. Sauté the fresh chopped mushrooms 5 minutes. Add the mushroom caps and cook 5 minutes. Remove the mushroom caps. Blend the flour into butter and mushroom stems mixture. Gradually add the cream and milk, stirring constantly until thickened, then add the salt and pepper. Add the dried mushrooms and the water. Cook 20 minutes.

Just before serving, add the sherry and the mushroom caps. Serve sprinkled with the parsley.

Serves 6

WATERZOOI DE POULET
(Belgian chicken-in-the-pot)

2 2-pound broilers, quartered	1 tablespoon salt
2 veal knuckles	1/2 teaspoon white pepper
6 cups water	3 slices lemon
2 stalks celery	2 cups dry white wine
1 parsnip	3 tablespoons butter
4 sprigs parsley	1/2 cup dry bread crumbs

Wash and dry the chicken and giblets. Combine the gizzards, livers, veal knuckles, celery, parsnips, parsley, salt, pepper, and lemon in a saucepan. Bring to a boil; cover, and cook over low heat 2 hours. Strain.

Combine the stock, wine, and butter in a casserole. Bring

to a boil and add the chicken; cover, and cook over low heat 30 minutes, or until chicken is tender. Stir in the bread crumbs, taste for seasoning, and serve directly from the casserole in deep bowls.

Serves 4-8

OXTAIL SOUP

1 oxtail	1 1/2 cups dry red wine
1/4 cup flour	6 cups water
3 tablespoons butter	2 teaspoons salt
1/2 pound ground beef	1/2 teaspoon freshly
1 cup chopped onion	ground black pepper
1/2 cup chopped celery	2 teaspoons paprika
1 tomato, peeled and	1 bay leaf
chopped	1/2 cup diced potatoes

Have the oxtail cut into 2-inch pieces. Wash, cover with water, and bring to a boil. Drain and dry. Roll in the flour.

Melt the butter in a saucepan; add the oxtail pieces, and cook until brown. Add the beef, onion, and celery, and continue browning. Mix in the tomato, wine, and 6 cups water, salt, pepper, paprika, bay leaf, and potato. Bring to a boil, cover, and cook over low heat 3 hours. Remove the oxtail pieces. Cut the meat from the bone into small pieces. Reserve. Discard the bones and bay leaf. Purée the soup in a blender, or force through a sieve. Return to saucepan, add the reserved meat, heat, and serve.

Serves 6-8

WEINSUPPE
(German wine soup)

3 egg whites	1/8 teaspoon ground
1/2 teaspoon salt	cloves
4 cups dry white wine	1 teaspoon sugar
1/4 teaspoon cinnamon	3 egg yolks

Beat the egg whites and salt until stiff. Drop by the heaping teaspoon into boiling water. Cook over low heat 5 minutes. Remove carefully with a slotted spoon.

While the egg whites are cooking, bring the wine, cinnamon, cloves, and sugar to a boil. Beat the egg yolks in a bowl; gradually add a little of the hot wine mixture, stirring steadily to prevent curdling. Return to the balance of the wine mixture. Heat, but do not let boil.

Serve the soup with the egg-white dumplings afloat.

Serves 4-6

TOMATO WINE SOUP

1 cup dry white wine	1 teaspoon sugar
3 cups beef broth	1/4 teaspoon freshly
4 cups tomato juice	ground black pepper
1/2 cup sliced onion	2 cloves
2 sprigs parsley	1/4 cup dry sherry
2 stalks celery	

Combine the wine, broth, tomato juice, onion slices, parsley, celery, sugar, pepper, and cloves in a saucepan. Bring to a boil, and cook over low heat 20 minutes. Strain, return to saucepan, and mix in the sherry. Taste for seasoning. Heat and serve in bouillon cups, with a slice of lemon sprinkled with paprika in each.

Serves 8-10

BISQUE DE HOMARD
(lobster bisque)

1 1/2-pound live lobster	1/4 teaspoon thyme
6 tablespoons butter	4 tablespoons flour
1/4 cup chopped onion	5 cups chicken broth
1/4 cup grated carrot	2 teaspoons salt
1/4 cup cognac	Dash cayenne pepper
3/4 cup dry sherry	1 1/2 cups heavy cream
1 cup bottled clam juice	

Have the lobster cut into 4 sections, shells and all, and the claws cracked. Melt half the butter in a saucepan; sauté the onion and carrot 5 minutes. Add the lobster; sauté 5 minutes, or until lobster turns red. Warm the cognac, pour over the lobster, and set aflame. When flames die, stir in the sherry, clam juice, and thyme. Cover and cook over low heat 15 minutes. Remove the lobster pieces; reserve the sauce. Scoop the lobster meat out of the shells and chop coarsely. Break up the lobster shells and pulverize in a blender with 2 tablespoons sauce, or put through a food chopper.

Melt the remaining butter in a saucepan; blend in the flour. Gradually add the chicken broth, stirring steadily to the boiling point. Add the salt, cayenne, reserved sauce, and pulverized shells. Cover, and cook over low heat 1 hour. Strain. Stir in the cream and lobster meat. Heat, and taste for seasoning.

Serves 6-8

SHRIMP–MUSHROOM BISQUE

4 tablespoons butter
2 pounds raw shrimp, shelled, deveined and diced
3/4 cup chopped mushrooms
2 cups bottled clam juice
2 cups dry white wine
1 stalk celery
1/8 teaspoon cayenne pepper
1/8 teaspoon nutmeg
1 cup heavy cream

Melt the butter in a saucepan; sauté the shrimp and mushrooms 5 minutes. Mix in the clam juice and wine. Add the celery, cayenne pepper, and nutmeg. Cook over low heat 20 minutes. Discard the celery, and purée the soup in a blender, or force through a food mill. Return to saucepan. Stir in the cream and season to taste. Heat, but do not let boil.

Serves 6-8

SOPA DE PESCADO
(shrimp and scallop soup)

6 tablespoons butter
1 cup finely chopped onion
4 cups bottled clam juice
4 cups dry white wine
1/2 teaspoon white pepper
1 cup diced white bread
1 cup milk
1 pound raw shrimp, shelled and deveined
1 pound scallops
1/8 teaspoon dried ground chili peppers
1/2 cup ground almonds
1 cup heavy cream
1/2 teaspoon paprika
2 hard-cooked eggs, chopped

Melt the butter in a saucepan; sauté the chopped onion until soft and lightly browned. Mix in the clam juice, wine, and pepper; bring to a boil, and cook over low heat 30 minutes. Soak the bread in the milk and mash smooth; add to soup in the saucepan and cook over low heat 10 minutes. Pour boiling water over the shrimp; drain. Add to the soup, with the scallops and chili peppers. Cook 5 minutes. Blend in the almonds, cream, paprika, and eggs. Cook 5 minutes longer. Taste for seasoning.

Serves 8-10

CIOPPINO
(San Francisco fish soup)

1 1/2-pound live lobster	1 29-ounce can tomatoes
24 small clams	2 8-ounce cans tomato
2 pounds red snapper,	sauce
sea bass, etc.	2 teaspoons salt
1 pound raw shrimp,	3/4 teaspoon freshly
shelled and deveined	ground black pepper
3/4 cup olive oil	1 bay leaf
1 1/2 cups chopped onion	2 cups dry red wine
1 cup diced green peppers	1/2 teaspoon oregano
3 cloves garlic, minced	

Have the lobster cut up in the shell, the bodies cut in half lengthwise, then in 3 pieces crosswise, and the claws in 2 pieces. Scrub the clams, and wash under cold running water for a few minutes. Cut the fish in bite-size pieces. Wash the shrimp. Keep all the fish refrigerated until needed.

Heat the oil in a heavy saucepan; sauté the chopped onions, green peppers, and garlic 10 minutes, stirring frequently. Add the tomatoes, tomato sauce, salt, and pepper. Cover and cook over low heat 2 hours, mixing frequently. Mix in the bay leaf, wine, and oregano; cook 10 minutes longer. Taste for seasoning.

Put all the fish and other seafood in a deep casserole; pour the sauce over it. Bring to a boil, cover, and cook over low heat 20 minutes. Serve in deep plates, with garlic toast.

Serve with an Italian red wine.

Serves 6-8

ZUPPA DI PESCE
(fish soup, Italian style)

3 pounds assorted sliced fish	1 1/2 cups chopped onion
1/3 cup olive oil	1 clove garlic, minced
1 1/2 teaspoon salt	2 tablespoons tomato paste
1/2 teaspoon black pepper	3 cups dry white wine
1 teaspoon finely chopped bay leaf	1 cup boiling water

Buy as many varieties of fish as possible, but be sure to include some eel. Cut the fish into serving-size pieces. Wash and dry.

Heat the oil in a heavy saucepan; brown the fish in it lightly. Season with the salt, pepper, and bay leaf; cook over low heat 15 minutes, turning the pieces once. Carefully remove the fish and keep warm. In the oil remaining in the pan, sauté the chopped onions 10 minutes. Mix in the garlic, tomato paste, and wine, then the boiling water. Cook over low heat 25 minutes. Return the fish to pan and cook 10 minutes longer. Taste for seasoning. Serve in deep plates with sautéed bread, rubbed with garlic. The resulting dish is a cross between a soup and a stew.

Serves 6-8

BOUILLABAISSE MARSEILLAISE
(fish soup, Marseille style)

1/3 cup olive oil	1/8 teaspoon saffron
1 1/2 cups chopped onion	2 pounds assorted fish, cut in serving-size pieces
2 cloves garlic, minced	1 lobster, cut up in the shell
2 cups chopped fresh tomatoes, or drained canned tomatoes	3/4 pound raw shrimp, shelled and deveined
2 cups dry white wine	1/2 pound scallops
2 cups bottled clam juice	12 mussels or clams, or both, scrubbed
1 bay leaf	2 tablespoons chopped parsley
1/2 teaspoon thyme	
1/8 teaspoon crushed fennel seeds	

Heat the oil in a large kettle; sauté the onion and garlic 5 minutes. Mix in the tomatoes, wine, clam juice, bay leaf, thyme, fennel, and saffron. Bring to a boil, and cook over low heat 30 minutes. Add the fish and other seafood. Cook 20 minutes longer. Taste for seasoning. Stir in the parsley. Serve in deep plates with garlic-rubbed toasted French bread.

Serves 6

TOMATO–CLAM BROTH

4 tablespoons butter
1 1/2 cups chopped onion
2 cups chopped tomatoes
1 clove garlic, minced
2 cups dry white wine

6 cups bottled clam juice
1/4 teaspoon white pepper
2 tablespoons minced parsley

Melt the butter in a saucepan; sauté the chopped onion 10 minutes. Add the tomatoes and garlic; cook over low heat 5 minutes. Mix in the wine, clam juice, and pepper. Cook over medium-low heat 30 minutes. Stir in the parsley, taste for seasoning, and serve with sautéed bread slices.

Serves 6-8

ZUPPA DI VONGOLE
(clam soup, Italian style)

48 small clams
3 cups dry white wine
1/2 cup olive oil
3/4 cup chopped onion
2 cloves garlic, minced
1/2 cup canned tomatoes, chopped

2 stalks celery
1/4 teaspoon marjoram
2 tablespoons minced parsley

Scrub the clams and wash under cold running water; combine in a kettle with the wine. Cover, and cook over high heat until clams open. Drain, reserving the stock. Remove the clams from the shells.

Heat the oil in a saucepan; sauté the onion until lightly browned. Add the garlic, tomatoes, celery, marjoram, and reserved stock. Cook over high heat 10 minutes. Discard the celery, and add the clams and parsley. Cook 1 minute. Serve in deep soup plates with croutons.

Serves 4-6

CREAM OF CLAM SOUP

2 10-ounce cans minced clams	2 tablespoons butter
3/4 cup dry white wine	2 egg yolks
1/4 teaspoon white pepper	1/2 cup heavy cream
	1 tablespoon minced parsley

Combine the undrained clams, the wine, pepper, and butter in a saucepan. Bring to a boil, and cook over heat 3 minutes.

Beat the egg yolks and cream in a bowl; gradually add some of the hot soup, stirring steadily to prevent curdling. Return to balance of soup and heat, stirring steadily, but do not let boil. Taste for seasoning. Serve immediately, sprinkled with the parsley.

Serves 4-5

MUSSEL CHOWDER

36 mussels	1 tablespoon thyme
1/2 cup water	3/4 cup white wine
1 large carrot, chopped	1 bay leaf
1 large onion, chopped	1 clove garlic
1 heaping tablespoon chopped parsley	Salt
1 green pepper, chopped	Freshly ground black pepper

Clean and scrub the mussels. Place them in a pot and steam them open with the water. Drain, reserving the liquid.

In another saucepan, combine the carrot, onion, parsley, green pepper, thyme, white wine, bay leaf, garlic, and the reserved liquid. Cook over low heat 45 minutes.

Add the mussels and cook 20 minutes. Discard the garlic and bay leaf, and add salt and pepper to taste. Serve in deep plates.

Serves 4-6

BILLI BI
(cream of mussel soup)

2 pounds mussels	Dash cayenne pepper
1 cup dry white wine	2 tablespoons butter
2 shallots, sliced	1 small bay leaf
2 onions, quartered	1/2 teaspoon thyme
2 sprigs parsley	1 egg yolk
1 teaspoon salt	2 cups heavy cream
1/4 teaspoon freshly ground black pepper	

Scrub the mussels well and wash under cold running water until water runs clear. Combine in a large pan with the wine, shallots, onions, parsley, salt, pepper, cayenne, butter, bay leaf, and thyme. Cover, and bring to a boil. Cook until the mussels have opened. Discard any mussels that do not open. Remove the mussels and discard the shells.

Strain the liquid through a double thickness of cheesecloth. Beat the egg yolk and cream; gradually add the mussel liquid, stirring steadily to prevent curdling.

Return to pan and cook, stirring steadily until thickened slightly, but do not let boil. Serve hot or ice-cold, garnished with the mussels.

Serves 4

TOMATO–CRAB SOUP

6 tablespoons butter	3 cups diced cooked tomatoes
1 cup chopped onion	Salt
4 tablespoons chopped celery	Pepper
5 tablespoons flour	3/4 pound crab meat, flaked
1 quart milk	1/2 cup dry sherry
1 pint light cream	

Melt the butter in a saucepan; sauté the onion and celery 10 minutes. Blend in the flour until smooth.

Gradually add the milk, stirring to the boiling point. Stir in the cream. Bring to a boil, and cook 5 minutes, stirring constantly. Purée the tomatoes in a blender, or force through a sieve. Add to the white sauce. Season with salt and pepper to taste. Add the crab meat and sherry; heat and serve.

Serves 8

CREAM OF KING CRAB SOUP

1 pound king crab (in shell)	1 tablespoon salt
3/4 cup diced onion	1/4 teaspoon white pepper
2 stalks celery, sliced	1/4 teaspoon thyme
4 tablespoons butter	1 1/2 cups light cream
4 tablespoons flour	1 1/2 cups dry white wine
1 1/2 quarts hot water	

If frozen crab is used, thaw it. Remove the meat and slice. Crush the shells. Sauté the shells, onion, and celery in the butter for 10 minutes. Blend in the flour; gradually add the water, salt, pepper, and thyme, stirring steadily to the boiling point. Cook over low heat 1 1/2 hours. Strain. Add the cream, wine, and crab meat. Cook 10 minutes. Taste for seasoning.

Serves 8-10

CHEESE SOUP

4 tablespoons butter	1/2 teaspoon salt
1/4 cup finely chopped onion	Dash cayenne pepper
1/2 cup grated carrot	1/2 cup dry sherry
1/4 cup chopped celery	2 cups (1/2 pound) grated Cheddar cheese
2 tablespoons flour	2 tablespoons chopped pimientos
2 cups chicken broth	

Melt the butter in a saucepan; sauté the onion, carrot, and celery 10 minutes, stirring frequently, but do not let brown. Blend in the flour; gradually add the broth, stirring steadily to the boiling point. Stir in the salt and cayenne pepper. Cook over low heat 10 minutes. Stir in the sherry, and the cheese until melted. Serve sprinkled with the pimientos.

Serves 4

OBSTSUPPE
(fruit soup)

1 pound plums	1/2 teaspoon cinnamon
1 pound peaches	1 tablespoon arrowroot
1/2 pound cherries	or cornstarch
4 cups water	2 tablespoons sweet
4 cups dry white wine	sherry
1 cup sugar	Whipped cream

Wash the fruit. Cut the plums and peaches in half, and discard the pits. Pit the cherries. Combine the fruits with the water, wine, sugar, and cinnamon. Bring to a boil, and cook over low heat 30 minutes, or until the fruits are very soft. Pureé in a blender, or force through a sieve. Return to the saucepan.

Mix the arrowroot with the sherry and stir into the soup. Cook over low heat, stirring steadily until thickened. Chill. Serve with a spoon of whipped cream in each plate.

Serves 6-8

COLD RED RASPBERRY SOUP

1 cup boiling water	1/4 cup sugar
1 quart fresh raspberries	1/3 cup orange juice
1 tablespoon cornstarch	1/2 cup dry sherry
2 tablespoons cold water	

Add the boiling water to the berries; cover, and cook 10 minutes. Force berries through a sieve. Mix cornstarch with cold water. Add with the sugar to hot pureé. Cook over low heat, stirring until mixture begins to thicken; cover, and cook over low heat 10 minutes. Cool slightly and mix in the orange juice. Chill. Add the sherry just before serving. Serve very cold, garnished with mint leaves.

Serves 4-6

FISH

CACIUCCO
(Leghorn fish stew)

3 pounds assorted salt-water fish
12 clams
1/2 cup olive oil
3/4 cup chopped onion
2 cloves garlic, minced
1 1/2 cups dry red wine
1 20-ounce can tomatoes, drained
1 1/2 teaspoons salt
1/2 teaspoon crushed dried red peppers
2 tablespoons minced parsley

Be sure the fish you buy is salt-water fish, and consists of more than one kind, cut in slices. Wash and dry the fish. Scrub the clams under cold running water until water runs clear.

Heat the oil in a saucepan; sauté the onion and garlic 5 minutes. Add the wine; cook until reduced to half. Mix in the tomatoes, salt, and red peppers. Arrange the sliced fish in it. Bring to a boil, and cook over low heat 25 minutes. Add the clams and parsley; cover, and cook 5 minutes longer, or until clams open. Discard any clams that do not open. Serve in deep plates with garlic toast.

Serve with a dry American white, a dry white Rhône wine like Hermitage Blanc or a Pouilly-Fuissé, or a *rosé*.

Serves 6-8

MATELOTE
(fish stew in white wine)

3 pounds assorted fresh-water fish
1 slice bacon
3 tablespoons butter
3 tablespoons olive oil
3 tablespoons flour
6 cups dry white wine
1 clove garlic, minced
2 teaspoons salt
1/4 teaspoon freshly ground black pepper
1 bay leaf, finely crushed
1/4 teaspoon marjoram
1/8 teaspoon nutmeg
2 tablespoons minced parsley
1/4 cup cognac
Sautéed French bread slices

Buy a varied assortment of fish, and include eel if possible.
Cut in serving-size pieces. Cover the bacon with water;
bring to a boil, then drain and chop coarsely.

Heat the butter and oil in a casserole; brown the bacon
in it. Stir in the flour until browned. Gradually add the
wine, stirring constantly to the boiling point. Mix in the
garlic, salt, pepper, bay leaf, marjoram, nutmeg, and parsley. Cover, and cook over low heat 30 minutes. Add the
fish and cook 20 minutes. Heat the cognac, set it aflame,
and pour it into the casserole; shake the casserole until
flames die. Arrange sautéed bread slices on top around
the edges of the casserole. Serve in deep plates.

Serve with a white New York State, a white Burgundy
like Chablis, a white Rhône wine like Hermitage Blanc, a
dry Loire Valley wine like Sancerre, or a *rosé*.

Serves 6-8

LA POCHOUSE BOURGUIGNONNE
(Burgundy fish stew)

4 pounds mixed fresh-
    water fish, after
    trimming
	2 cloves garlic, minced

	1 teaspoon meat extract
	4 tablespoons flour
1/4 pound (1 stick) butter	2 1/2 teaspoons salt
2 tablespoons diced bacon	1/2 teaspoon freshly ground pepper
2 quarts dry white wine	1/2 cup cognac
1 bay leaf } tied	Sautéed French bread
6 sprigs parsley } together	slices
1/2 teaspoon thyme	

Four or more types of fish are needed for this dish. Pike,
trout, carp, white fish, and eel are good choices. Cut the
fish into pieces 1 1/2 inches thick. Melt 6 tablespoons
butter in a deep saucepan, add the bacon, and sauté until
browned. Add the wine, bay leaf and parsley, thyme, and
garlic; bring to a boil. Cook over low heat 20 minutes.
Add fish and cook over medium heat 20 minutes. Blend
in the meat extract, and the flour kneaded with the remaining butter. Add salt and pepper; taste for seasoning.
Set the cognac aflame and add, shaking pan till flames die
down.

Put the sautéed bread slices (rubbed with garlic, if you like) in the bottom of a deep tureen, and pour the soup over it. Serve at once.

Serves 8-10

CAZUELA DE MARISCOS
(mixed seafood casserole)

1/4 cup olive oil
1 1/2 cups chopped onion
1 cup julienne-cut green peppers
1 1/2 cups peeled, diced potatoes
2 teaspoons salt
1/2 teaspoon freshly ground black pepper
1 clove garlic, minced
2 teaspoons finely chopped bay leaves
1 1/2 cups dry white wine

4 tablespoons tomato paste
1 cup boiling water
1 pound fillet of sole, cut in bite-size pieces
1 pound raw shrimp, shelled and deveined
1/2 pound crab meat
2 tablespoons minced parsley
Sautéed French or Italian bread slices

Heat the oil in a casserole; sauté the onion 10 minutes. Add the green peppers and potatoes; cook 5 minutes. Mix in the salt, pepper, garlic, bay leaves, wine, tomato paste, and boiling water. Cover, and cook over low heat 20 minutes. Add the fillet of sole; cook 15 minutes. Mix in the shrimp and crab meat; cook 10 minutes. Taste for seasoning. Sprinkle with the parsley. Arrange sautéed bread around the edge of the casserole.

Serve with a white Burgundy, a dry German white wine, a Loire Valley wine like Pouilly-Fumé, a *rosé*, or a white American wine.

Serves 6-8

CAZUELA DE PESCADO
(fish, potato, and rice casserole)

1/2 cup raw long-grain rice
1/2 cup olive oil

2 cups thinly sliced onion
2 cups thinly sliced potatoes

2 pounds fillets of fish,
    cut in 2-inch pieces
2 teaspoons salt
3/4 teaspoon freshly
    ground black pepper

1 cup diced tomatoes
1 1/2 cups dry white
    wine
1 cup bottled clam juice

Wash the rice under cold running water until water runs clear. Grease a casserole with 2 tablespoons of the oil. Spread half the sliced onions on the bottom with half the sliced potatoes over them. Spread the fish over the potatoes; sprinkle with half the salt and pepper. Cover the fish with the remaining onions, then the remaining potatoes, the rice, and tomatoes. Sprinkle with the remaining salt and pepper. Add the wine and clam juice. Cover, and bake in a 350° oven 1 hour, removing the cover for the last 10 minutes.

Serve with a white American wine, a white Burgundy, especially a Chablis, a Rhône wine like Hermitage Blanc, as Alsatian white wine like Sylvaner, or a *rosé*.

Serves 6-8

CASSEROLE DE POISSON
(fish casserole)

4 slices bacon
6 fillets sole
2 1/2 teaspoons salt
3/4 teaspoon freshly
    ground black pepper
1 1/2 cups chopped
    onion
1 cup grated carrot
1/2 pound mushrooms,
    sliced

3 tablespoons minced
    parsley
1/2 cup peeled, chopped
    tomatoes
1/2 teaspoon thyme
1/2 cup diced cooked
    ham
1 cup dry white wine
3 tablespoons butter

Fry the bacon until it begins to brown. Drain and crumble.

Cut the fillets in half. Season with 1 1/2 teaspoons of the salt and 1/4 teaspoon pepper. Spread the bacon on the bottom of a shallow greased casserole. Mix together the onion, carrot, mushrooms, parsley, tomatoes, thyme, remaining salt and pepper, and ham. Spread half the mixture over the bacon. Arrange the fish over the vegetables and cover with remaining vegetable mixture. Add the wine, and dot with the butter. Bake in a 375° oven 45 minutes.

Serve with a New York State white wine, a white Burgundy, a dry German white wine, an Alsatian wine like Riesling, or any rosé.

Serves 6-8

LOBSTER AND MACARONI CASSEROLE

1/4 pound (1 stick) butter
1/2 cup grated onion
1 clove garlic, minced
4 tablespoons flour
2 cups chicken broth
2 tablespoons tomato
    paste
1 1/2 cups dry white
    wine
1 pound cooked lobster
    meat, diced

1/4 cup chopped parsley
1 teaspoon salt
1/2 teaspoon freshly
    ground black pepper
1 pound elbow macaroni,
    cooked, and drained
1/2 cup grated Swiss
    cheese
1 teaspoon paprika

Melt half the butter in a saucepan; sauté the onion and garlic 5 minutes, stirring frequently. Blend in the flour. Gradually add the broth, stirring constantly to the boiling point. Mix in the tomato paste. Cook over low heat for 15 minutes. Add the wine, lobster, parsley, salt, and pepper. Cook over low heat for 5 minutes. Mix in the macaroni and taste for seasoning.

Pour the mixture into a buttered casserole. Sprinkle with the cheese and paprika. Dot with the remaining butter. Bake in a 375° oven 20 minutes, or until lightly browned.

Serve with a white American, a white Burgundy, champagne, a dry German white wine, or an Italian white wine like Orvieto.

Serves 4-6

TROUT WITH WINE ASPIC

4 brook trout
2 cups dry white wine
3/4 cup water
1 1/2 teaspoon salt
1/4 teaspoon white
   pepper

1 tablespoon minced
   parsley
1/4 teaspoon tarragon
1 envelope (tablespoon)
   gelatin
3 tablespoons dry sherry

Wash the trout; remove the heads if you like.

In a skillet, combine the wine, water, salt, pepper, parsley, and tarragon. Bring to a boil, and cook over low heat 10 minutes. Arrange the trout in the skillet. Bring to a boil, cover loosely, and cook over low heat 20 minutes, or until the fish flakes easily when tested with a fork. Carefully transfer the trout to a serving dish.

Soften the gelatin in the sherry, then stir into the hot stock until dissolved. Pour over the fish and chill until set.

Serve with a dry German white wine, or a Loire Valley wine like Pouilly-Fumé, or a *rosé*.

Serves 4

SPAGHETTI WITH ONIONS AND ANCHOVIES

1/2 cup olive oil
1 1/2 pounds onion,
   chopped
8 anchovies, chopped
1 8-ounce can tomato
   sauce

1/2 cup dry white wine
1 teaspoon oregano
1/2 cup chopped parsley
1 pound spaghetti, cooked
   and drained

Heat the olive oil in a saucepan; sauté the chopped onions 10 minutes, stirring frequently. Mix in the anchovies, tomato sauce, wine and oregano. Cook over low heat 45 minutes. Add a little water if the sauce is too thick. Add the parsley. Taste for seasoning.

Heap the spaghetti on a platter and pour the sauce over it. Toss lightly and serve immediately.

Serve with a dry Italian white wine like Verdicchio or Orvieto, a dry white Bordeaux wine, or with a dry American white wine.

Serves 4-6

BAKED FISH AND MACARONI

2 cups water	1/2 teaspoon freshly
1 1/4 cups dry white	ground black pepper
wine	1/2 cup heavy cream
1/2 cup chopped carrot	1 egg yolk
1/2 cup chopped onion	1/2 pound elbow
2 teaspoons salt	macaroni, cooked
2 pounds white fish or	and drained
sea bass	1/4 cup grated Swiss
2 tablespoons butter	cheese
2 tablespoons flour	3 tablespoons dry bread
1 teaspoon salt	crumbs

Bring the water and 1 cup of the wine to a boil; add the carrot, onion, salt, and fish. Cover, and cook over low heat 15 minutes. Drain. Strain, and reserve 1 1/2 cups stock. Remove skin and bones and cut fish into 2-inch pieces.

Melt the butter in a saucepan, blend in the flour, salt, and pepper. Add fish stock and cream, stirring steadily until sauce thickens. Beat the egg yolk and remaining wine in a bowl. Add the hot sauce, stirring steadily to prevent curdling. In a 2-quart buttered baking dish, spread a layer of macaroni, sprinkle with some grated cheese, add a layer of fish, and then a layer of sauce. Repeat until all ingredients are used up. Have the top layer macaroni. Sprinkle with the bread crumbs and bake in a preheated 400° oven 20 minutes.

Serve with any dry white wine, or if you wish, with a rosé.

Serves 6

SEAFOOD KABOBS

30 scallops	1/4 teaspoon dry mustard
1 cup soy sauce	1/4 teaspoon thyme
2/3 cup dry red wine	1 teaspoon ground ginger
1/4 cup sherry	1 teaspoon Worcestershire
1/2 cup pineapple juice	sauce
1/2 cup brown sugar	30 shrimp, cooked and
1/4 cup melted butter	cleaned

Cover the scallops with water; bring to a boil and drain.

In a bowl, combine the soy sauce, red wine, sherry, pineapple juice, sugar, butter, mustard, thyme, ginger, and Worcestershire sauce. Marinate the scallops and shrimp in the mixture for 2 hours. Arrange the shrimp and scallops alternately on 6, 8 or 10 skewers.

Broil 3 minutes on each side. Serve with boiled rice and sautéed pineapple slices.

Serve with a dry American white wine.

Serves 6-10

FILETS DE POISSON EN SOUFFLÉ

1/2 cup dry vermouth	3 tablespoons flour
1/4 cup sliced onion	1 cup milk, scalded
1 1/8 teaspoons salt	Dash nutmeg
1/4 teaspoon white pepper	1 egg yolk
	4 egg whites
1/2 pound fillet of sole	1/2 cup grated Swiss
3 tablespoons butter	cheese

Combine the vermouth, sliced onion, 1/2 teaspoon of the salt, and 1/4 teaspoon pepper in a skillet. Bring to a boil, and add the fish fillets. Cover, and cook over low heat 10 minutes. Drain, and flake the fish coarsely.

Melt the butter in a saucepan; blend in the flour. Add the milk, stirring steadily to the boiling point. Add the nutmeg, 1/2 teaspoon of the remaining salt, and the remaining pepper; cook over low heat 5 minutes. Beat the egg yolk in a bowl; gradually add the hot sauce, stirring steadily to prevent curdling. Cool.

Beat the egg whites and remaining salt until stiff but not dry. Stir about 1/4 of this into the sauce, mix in 1/3 cup of the cheese, then fold in the remaining egg whites.

Use 6 individual shallow baking dishes. Spread each with about a 1/4-inch layer of the soufflé mixture. Put the fish over it and heap the remaining soufflé mixture over the fish. Sprinkle with the remaining cheese. Bake in a preheated 425° oven (on upper rack) 15 minutes, or until puffed and browned. Serve immediately.

Serve with a dry American, a dry white Burgundy, such

as a Chablis, a dry German white wine, or a dry Italian white wine like Orvieto.

Serves 6

BAKED FILLET OF SOLE

1 1/2 cups champagne or dry white wine
2 tablespoons butter
2 tablespoons grated onion
1 bay leaf
1/2 cup chopped mushrooms
2 teaspoons chopped parsley
3 tablespoons heavy cream
2 tablespoons salt
1 1/2 teaspoons white pepper
4 fillets of sole
2 tablespoons grated Parmesan cheese

Combine the champagne or white wine, butter, onion, bay leaf, mushrooms, and parsley in a saucepan. Bring to a boil, and cook over medium heat 10 minutes. Mix in the cream. Discard the bay leaf.

Sprinkle the salt and pepper on the fillets. Arrange in a buttered baking dish in a single layer. Pour the sauce over them and sprinkle with the cheese. Bake in a 375° oven 25 minutes.

Serve with a dry German white wine, a white Burgundy, a dry white Bordeaux, a *rosé*, or a dry American white wine.

Serves 4

FILLET OF SOLE WITH MUSHROOM–HOLLANDAISE SAUCE

6 fillets of sole
2 teaspoons salt
1/4 teaspoon white pepper
1/2 cup chopped onion
1/4 cup dry white wine
6 tablespoons butter
1 tablespoon flour
2 cups Hollandaise sauce (see recipe)
1/2 cup whipped cream
1/2 cup chopped mushrooms
1/2 cup minced pimientos
3/4 cup peeled chopped tomatoes

Cut each fillet in thirds lengthwise and roll up. Fasten with toothpicks if necessary. Season with salt and pepper. Arrange in a buttered baking pan; sprinkle with the chopped onion and wine. Cover with buttered aluminum foil and bake in a 350° oven 15 minutes. Transfer to a shallow ovenproof serving dish. Knead the flour in 3 tablespoons butter, and add to the wine sauce remaining in the pan. Bring to a boil, and cook until thickened. Strain. Add the Hollandaise sauce and whipped cream.

Sauté the mushrooms, pimientos, and tomatoes in the remaining butter for 5 minutes. Spread over the fish and cover with the sauce. Bake in a 400° oven 5 minutes, or until delicately browned. Serve with parsley potatoes.

Serve with any American white or *rosé* wine.

Serves 6-8

HOMARD À L'AMERICAINE
(lobster Americaine)

2 1 1/2-pound live lobsters	1 carrot, grated
3 tablespoons olive oil	3 tablespoons cognac
1 1/4 teaspoons salt	1 bay leaf
1/2 teaspoon freshly ground black pepper	1 cup peeled, chopped tomatoes
3 tablespoons butter	3/4 cup dry white wine
1/2 cup chopped onion	1 clove garlic, minced
	1/2 teaspoon thyme

Have the bodies of the lobsters cut into 4 pieces crosswise and the claws cracked. Scoop out the liver (tomalley) and reserve.

Heat the oil in a skillet; add the lobster, salt, and pepper and cook 5 minutes, or until lobsters turn red. (At this point the lobster meat may be removed from the shells, if you like.)

Melt 2 tablespoons butter in a deep casserole; sauté the onion and carrot until browned. Add the lobster pieces. Heat the cognac in a ladle, pour over the lobster, and set aflame. When flames die, stir in the bay leaf, tomatoes, wine, garlic, and thyme. Cover tightly, and cook over low heat 20 minutes. Cream the remaining butter with the reserved liver and stir into the sauce. Cook 5 minutes. Taste for seasoning. If lobster meat has not been removed from the shells earlier, it may now be removed before serving, if desired.

Serve with a white American wine, a white Burgundy, a Loire Valley wine like Chinon, or a *rosé*.

Serves 2-4

ARAGOSTA FRA DIAVOLO
(lobster in tomato sauce)

2 1 1/2-pound live
  lobsters or 4 African
  lobster tails
1/2 cup olive oil
3/4 cup chopped onion
1 clove garlic, minced
1 1/2 teaspoons salt
1/4 teaspoon crushed
  dried red peppers

1 pound tomatoes, peeled
  and chopped
1 tablespoon tomato
  paste
3/4 cup dry white wine
1/2 teaspoon oregano
2 tablespoons minced
  parsley

Have the lobsters cut up in the shell, the bodies in half lengthwise, and then in 3 pieces, and the claws cracked; or cut the lobster tails in 3 pieces crosswise.

Heat the oil in a large deep skillet; cook the lobster over high heat 3 minutes. Add the onion, garlic, salt, and dried peppers; cook until lobsters turn red, about 3 minutes. Mix in the tomatoes and tomato paste; cook 2 minutes. Add the wine and oregano. Cook over medium heat 10 minutes. Sprinkle with the parsley and serve.

Serve with a white Burgundy, a dry Italian white wine like Orvieto, or, if you wish, with any Italian red wine like Chianti, or a California red wine.

Serves 2-4

LOBSTER IN SPICY SAUCE

3 1 1/2-pound live
  lobsters
1/2 cup olive oil
1 1/2 cups chopped
  onion

2 cloves garlic, minced
1/3 cup cognac
1 3/4 teaspoons salt
1/2 teaspoon freshly
  ground black pepper

3 tablespoons tomato
   paste
1 teaspoon meat extract
1/4 teaspoon thyme
1/4 teaspoon saffron

1 cup dry white wine
1 teaspoon prepared
   mustard
2 tablespoons minced
   parsley

Have the lobsters cut up, bodies in thirds and claws in half. Heat the oil in a deep skillet or casserole; add the lobster pieces, and cook over high heat 5 minutes. Remove the lobster pieces and pour off half the oil. (If you like, the shells may be discarded at this point.) Sauté the onion and garlic in the oil remaining in the pan 5 minutes. Return the lobster pieces to the pan. Warm the cognac, set aflame, and pour over the lobster. When flames die, season with the salt and pepper. Mix together the tomato paste, meat extract, thyme, saffron, and wine. Mix in the lobster pieces. Cover and cook over medium heat 15 minutes. Arrange lobster pieces on a heated serving dish. Stir the mustard and parsley into the sauce. Pour over the lobster.

Serve with a dry white Burgundy, a *rosé*, or an American white or *rosé* wine.

Serves 2-4

HOMARD AU PORTO
(lobster in port)

2 1 1/4-pound live
   lobsters
5 tablespoons butter
3/4 cup chopped onion
1/2 cup grated carrot
1 teaspoon salt

1/4 teaspoon white
   pepper
3/4 cup port
2 tablespoons flour
3/4 cup heavy cream

Have the lobsters cut up, bodies in thirds and claws in half. Remove the meat of the bodies and claws, and slice. Melt 4 tablespoons butter in a saucepan; sauté the onion and carrot 5 minutes. Add the lobster meat; sauté 3 minutes, turning the pieces to coat all sides. Add the salt, pepper, and port. Cook over low heat 15 minutes. Transfer lobster to a heated serving dish and keep hot. Mix the flour and cream until smooth; add to the sauce with the remaining butter, stirring constantly to the boiling point.

Cook over low heat 5 minutes. Taste for seasoning, and strain over the lobster meat.

Serve with a white American wine, a white Burgundy, a dry Italian white wine, a German white wine, or a *rosé*.

Serves 2-4

HOMARD À LA NEWBURG
(lobster newburg)

4 tablespoons butter	3/4 cup sweet sherry
1 pound cooked lobster meat, sliced	4 egg yolks
	1 cup heavy cream
1 teaspoon salt	
1/4 teaspoon white pepper	

Melt the butter in a deep skillet; add the lobster, salt, and pepper and sauté 2 minutes, stirring a few times. Stir in the sherry; cook over low heat until wine is almost evaporated. Just before serving, beat together the egg yolks and cream; add to the lobster, stirring steadily until thickened, but do not let boil. Taste for seasoning.

Serve with a white Burgundy, a *rosé*, or an American white or *rosé* wine.

Serves 4-6

HOMARD THERMIDOR
(lobster thermidor)

2 cups dry white wine	3 tablespoons dry vermouth
4 cups water	1/4 teaspoon chervil
1 onion	1/4 teaspoon dry mustard
1 bay leaf	1/8 teaspoon tarragon
1 stalk celery	1/4 teaspoon white pepper
3 teaspoons salt	
2 1 1/2-pound live lobsters	1 tablespoon beef extract
1/4 pound butter	4 tablespoons grated Parmesan cheese
4 tablespoons flour	
2 cups light cream	

Combine the white wine, water, onion, bay leaf, celery, and 2 teaspoons salt in a saucepan; bring to a boil, and cook over low heat 20 minutes. Plunge the lobsters into boiling liquid and cook 20 minutes. Remove lobsters, drain, cool, and split. Remove the meat of the bodies and claws; slice. Reserve the body shells. Pour off all but 1 cup of the lobster stock; cook over high heat until reduced to 1/4 cup.

Melt 4 tablespoons butter in a saucepan; blend in the flour and remaining salt. Gradually add the cream, stirring steadily to the boiling point. Mix in the vermouth, chervil, mustard, tarragon, pepper, beef extract, and reduced stock. Cook over low heat 5 minutes. Taste for seasoning and stir in the remaining butter. Spread a little of the sauce on the bottom of the reserved shells and arrange the lobster meat over it. Cover with remaining sauce and sprinkle with the cheese. Place under the broiler until browned.

Serve with a white American, a white Burgundy, a Loire Valley white wine, or a *rosé*.

Serves 2-4

HOMARD AU CHAMPAGNE
(lobster in champagne sauce)

4 tablespoons butter	1 cup heavy cream
3/4 cup sliced blanched almonds	1 teaspoon salt
	Dash cayenne pepper
2 tablespoons flour	2 pounds cooked lobster meat, cubed
2 cups champagne or dry white wine	1 tablespoon chopped parsley
2 egg yolks	

Melt 2 tablespoons of the butter in a skillet. Add the almonds. Sauté until brown, stirring almost constantly.

Melt the remaining butter in a saucepan. Blend in the flour until smooth. Gradually add the champagne or white wine, stirring constantly to the boiling point, then cook over low heat 5 minutes.

Beat the egg yolks, cream, salt, and cayenne pepper in a bowl. Gradually add 1 cup of the champagne sauce, beating constantly to prevent curdling. Return the mixture to the balance of the sauce. Fold in the lobster meat and almonds. Taste for seasoning. Reheat, but do not allow to boil. Sprinkle with the parsley. Serve with boiled rice.

Serve with champagne, a dry American or German white wine, a white Burgundy, or any dry Italian white wine like Orvieto.

Serves 6-8

COQUILLES SAINT-JACQUES
(baked scallops)

1 pound scallops	6 tablespoons butter
1 1/2 cups water	3 tablespoons flour
3/4 cup dry white wine	2 egg yolks
2 sprigs parsley } tied	4 tablespoons heavy
1 bay leaf } together	cream
1/2 pound mushrooms,	1 1/4 teaspoons salt
chopped	1/4 teaspoon white
1 cup finely chopped	pepper
onion	1/2 cup dry bread
2 tablespoons sherry	crumbs
1 teaspoon lemon juice	

Combine the scallops, 1 1/2 cups water, the wine, parsley, and bay leaf in a saucepan; bring to a boil, and cook over low heat 5 minutes. Drain scallops, reserve the liquid. In a saucepan combine the mushrooms, onion, sherry, lemon juice, and 2 tablespoons butter. Bring to a boil, cover, and cook 10 minutes. Strain and reserve the liquid. Dice the scallops.

Melt 3 tablespoons butter in a saucepan; blend in the flour. Add the reserved liquids, stirring constantly to the boiling point. Cook over low heat 3 minutes. Beat the egg yolks and cream in a bowl, and mix in a little of the hot sauce, stirring steadily to prevent curdling. Return to balance of sauce and cook until thickened; do not allow to boil. Season with the salt and pepper. Add the scallops to sauce with the mushroom-onion mixture. Mix well, and spoon into 6 scallop shells or ramekins. Sprinkle with the bread crumbs and dot with remaining butter. Bake in a 425° oven 10 minutes.

Serve with a dry white Burgundy, a Loire Valley wine like Chinon, an Alsatian wine, or a white American wine.

Serves 6

COQUILLES ST.-JACQUES MARINÉES
(marinated broiled scallops)

1 1/2 pounds scallops
1/2 cup olive oil
1/2 cup dry vermouth
2 cloves garlic, minced

2 tablespoons minced
   parsley
3/4 teaspoon salt

If sea scallops are used, cut in half crosswise. If bay scallops are used, leave whole. Wash and dry. Combine the oil, vermouth, garlic, parsley, and salt in a glass or pottery bowl. Marinate the scallops in mixture 4 hours, or overnight, in the refrigerator.

Arrange scallops in a shallow pan with marinade. Broil 2 inches from heat until golden brown, turning to brown all sides.

To serve as hot hors d'oeuvre, pierce with cocktail picks.

Serve with any dry white wine, especially an Italian white wine.

Serves 4-6

RISOTTO DI SCAMPI
(shrimp risotto)

3 tablespoons olive oil
6 tablespoons butter
1 clove garlic, minced
1 1/2 cups raw rice
3/4 cup dry white wine
4 cups hot chicken broth
1 pound cooked shrimp,
   shelled and deveined

1 1/2 teaspoons salt
1/4 teaspoon white
   pepper
1/4 teaspoon marjoram
3 tablespoons grated
   Parmesan cheese

Heat the oil and 4 tablespoons of the butter in a heavy deep skillet or a casserole. Add the garlic and rice; cook until rice is translucent, stirring frequently. Add the wine; cook over medium heat until absorbed. Add half the broth; cover, and cook over low heat 15 minutes. Mix in the shrimp, salt, pepper, marjoram, and remaining broth. Re-cover, and cook 10 minutes longer, or until rice is tender and dry. Stir in the cheese and remaining butter with a fork.

Serve with any dry white wine, especially a Loire Valley wine or a white Burgundy.

Serves 4-6

DEVILED SHRIMP

2 pounds raw shrimp, shelled and deveined
1 cup dry white wine
1/4 cup cognac
3 sprigs parsley
1 carrot, sliced
1 onion
1 clove garlic, split
1 1/2 teaspoons salt
1/4 teaspoon thyme
1 bay leaf
2 tablespoons heavy cream
2 tablespoons dry sherry
1 cup mayonnaise
1/4 cup chopped pimiento-stuffed olives

Wash and drain the shrimp. Combine the wine, cognac, parsley, carrot, onion, garlic, salt, thyme, and bay leaf in a saucepan. Bring to a boil, add the shrimp, and cook over low heat 8 minutes. Let cool in the liquid. Drain thoroughly.

Blend the cream and sherry with the mayonnaise; fold in the chopped olives. Arrange the shrimp on a platter or on individual dishes and cover with the mayonnaise mixture. Or if you want to serve the shrimp as an hors d'eouvre, serve the mayonnaise mixture as a dip.

Serve with a dry white American wine, a dry German whtie wine, or a Loire Valley wine like Pouilly-Fumé.

Serves 4-6

POISSON AUX OLIVES
(fish with olives)

2 pounds sea bass or mackerel, split
1 1/2 teaspoons salt
1/4 teaspoon white pepper
1/4 cup olive oil
1/4 cup dry white wine
1/4 teaspoon thyme
1/8 teaspoon finely chopped bay leaf
1/2 cup pitted black olives
Orange slices

Wash and dry the fish. Season with the salt and pepper. Rub a baking dish with a little oil and arrange the fish in it. Pour the oil and wine over it, and sprinkle with the thyme and bay leaf. Bake in a 375° oven 20 minutes, basting occasionally. Add the olives and bake 5 minutes longer. Garnish with orange slices. Serve hot or cold.

Serve with a white Burgundy, a white American wine a white Rhône wine like Châteauneuf-du-Pape Blanc, a dry Italian white wine like Soave, or a *rosé*.

Serves 4

FILETS DE MAQUEREAUX AU VIN BLANC
(mackerel in white wine)

2 2-pound mackerel, filleted	6 peppercorns
1 1/2 cups dry white wine	1 bay leaf
	1/8 teaspoon fennel
1/4 cup water	1 teaspoon prepared French mustard
3/4 cup sliced onion	
1 1/4 teaspoons salt	2 tablespoons minced parsley

Remove all the bones of the fish; wash and dry. Cut each fillet in half lengthwise, and then crosswise.

In a skillet, combine and bring to a boil the wine, water, sliced onion, salt, peppercorns, bay leaf and fennel. Cook over low heat 15 minutes. Arrange the fish in it; cook over low heat 10 minutes. Cool the fish for 15 minutes in the stock then transfer fish to a deep dish. Strain the liquid and measure 1 cup; mix in the mustard and parsley. Pour over the fish. Chill 24 hours before serving.

Serve with a white American wine, a white Rhône wine like Hermitage Blanc, a dry Italian white wine like Orvieto, or a *rosé*.

Serves 4-6

SHERRIED TUNA

4 tablespoons butter	1/2 cup dry sherry
3 tablespoons grated onion	2 7 3/4-ounce cans tuna fish, drained and flaked
4 tablespoons flour	
2 cups milk	
1 teaspoon salt	1/2 cup sliced pimiento-stuffed olives
1/4 teaspoon white pepper	

Melt the butter in a saucepan; sauté the grated onion 3 minutes. Blend in the flour. Gradually add the milk, stirring steadily to the boiling point. Stir in the salt, pepper, and sherry; cook over low heat 5 minutes. Add the tuna fish and sliced olives; cook 3 minutes. Taste for seasoning. Serve on rice or toast, or in patty shells.

Serve with a *rosé* wine.

Serves 6

POACHED SALMON STEAK

2 tablespoons butter	2 teaspoons salt
1/2 cup onion	1/4 teaspoon white
1/3 cup grated carrot	pepper
1/3 cup chopped celery	1 bay leaf
3 cups water	1 3-pound salmon steak
1/2 cup dry white wine	

Melt the butter in a large skillet; sauté the onion, carrot, and celery 5 minutes. Add the water, wine, salt, pepper, and bay leaf; bring to a boil and cook 5 minutes. Carefully lower the salmon into the liquid. Cover loosely, and cook over low heat 40 minutes. Remove the salmon carefully, and serve hot with Hollandaise sauce, or cold with mayonnaise.

Serve with a white or *rosé* American wine.

Serves 6

BAKED SALMON STEAKS

4 slices salmon, 1 inch thick	3/4 cup chopped onion
2 teaspoons salt	1/4 cup grated carrot
1/2 teaspoon freshly ground black pepper	2 tablespoons flour
3 tablespoons butter	2 cups dry white wine
	1 bay leaf
	3 sprigs parsley

Wash and dry the fish. If the slices are large, cut each in half through the bone. Season with the salt and pepper. In a large skillet, melt the butter. Sauté the onion and carrot 5 minutes. Blend in the flour; gradually add the wine, stirring steadily to the boiling point. If skillet has an ovenproof handle, arrange the fish in it. If not, pour the sauce into a baking dish and arrange the fish in it. Add the bay leaf and parsley. Cover the fish with a piece of buttered aluminum foil. Bake in a 400° oven 40 minutes, or until fish flakes easily when tested with a fork. Transfer the fish to a heated serving dish. Taste the sauce for seasoning, and pour over the fish.

Serve with a white American wine, a Bordeaux wine, a dry German white wine, or a *rosé*.

Serves 4

BAKED STUFFED RED SNAPPER

1 4-pound red snapper, split and boned for stuffing	3/4 cup chopped onion
	3 cups dry bread crumbs
	1 cup chopped cucumber
2 teaspoons salt	2 teaspoons capers
1/2 teaspoon freshly ground black pepper	1/4 teaspoon marjoram
	1/2 cup dry white wine
3/8 pound (1 1/2 sticks) butter	6 slices bacon

Sprinkle the fish inside and out with 1 1/2 teaspoons of the salt and 1/4 teaspoon pepper.

Heat half the butter in a skillet; sauté the chopped onion 5 minutes. Mix in the bread crumbs, cucumber, capers, marjoram, half the wine, and remaining salt and pepper. Stuff the fish, and close opening with skewers or toothpicks.

Place the fish in a buttered shallow baking pan. Cut 6 gashes on the top and place a piece of bacon in each. Dot with the remaining butter, and pour the remaining wine over the top.

Bake in a 400° oven 5 minutes, or until the fish flakes easily when tested with a fork. Baste frequently with the pan juices.

Serve with any American white or *rosé* wine.

Serves 6

MORUE EN VIN ROUGE
(salt cod in red wine)

2 pounds salt cod
1/2 cup flour
3/4 cup olive oil
3/4 cup finely chopped
    onion
1 1/2 cups dry red wine
1 cup water
1 tablespoon tomato
    paste

1/2 teaspoon freshly
    ground black pepper
1 bay leaf
1/4 teaspoon thyme
2 tablespoons minced
    parsley
2 tablespoons capers

Wash the codfish, cover with cold water, and let soak 12 hours, changing the water a few times. Drain, cover with fresh water, and bring to a boil. Drain, remove the skin and bones, and cut fish into squares. Roll the squares in the flour (reserving 1 1/2 tablespoons). Heat 1/2 cup of the oil in a skillet; brown the squares in it. Pour off the oil and set fish aside. Wipe the skillet clean with paper towels.

Heat the remaining oil in the skillet; sauté the onion 10 minutes. Blend in the reserved flour until golden. Add the wine and water, stirring steadily to the boiling point. Mix in the tomato paste, pepper, bay leaf, thyme, and parsley. Bring to a boil, and cook over low heat 30 minutes. Add the codfish and capers; cook 15 minutes longer. Taste for seasoning, discard the bay leaf, and serve on sautéed bread slices or boiled rice.

Serve with a red Burgundy like Beaujolais, a dry white Burgundy, or an American rosé.

Serves 6-8

ANGUILLES, SAUCE VERT
(eels in green sauce)

1 1/2 pounds eels
1/2 cup olive oil
2 cups boiling chicken
    broth
1 cup dry white wine
2 tablespoons lemon juice
1 teaspoon salt

1/4 teaspoon freshly
    ground black pepper
1/4 cup cooked puréed
    spinach
1/4 cup chopped parsley
1/4 cup chopped mint
1/4 cup chopped chives

Clean the eels, remove the skin, and cut in 1 1/2-inch lengths.

Heat the oil in a skillet; sauté the eels 5 minutes. Add the broth, and cook 5 minutes longer. Drain.

Combine the eels, wine, lemon juice, salt, pepper, spinach, parsley, mint, and chives. Bring to a boil. Cool and chill.

Serve with any dry American white wine.

Serves 8-10

POLLO ALLA CACCIATORA
(chicken in red wine, hunter's style)

5-pound roasting chicken, disjointed
1/4 cup olive oil
3/4 cup chopped onion
3/4 cup thinly sliced green peppers
1 clove garlic, minced
1 1/2 teaspoons salt
1/2 teaspoon black pepper
1/4 teaspoon rosemary
3/4 cup peeled, chopped tomatoes
1 cup dry red wine
1/4 pound mushrooms, sliced
2 tablespoons butter

Wash and dry the chicken pieces. Heat the oil in a Dutch oven or deep skillet; brown the chicken in it. Mix in the onion, green peppers, garlic, salt, pepper, and rosemary; cook 10 minutes. Mix in the tomatoes and wine; bring to a boil, cover, and cook over low heat 30 minutes. Sauté the mushrooms in the butter 5 minutes. Add to the chicken; re-cover, and cook 10 minutes longer, or until the chicken is tender. Taste for seasoning.

Serve with an Italian red wine like Chianti, a red Bordeaux, or a red Burgundy, especially Beaujolais, or an American red wine.

Serves 4-6

POULET AU CHAMPAGNE
(chicken in champagne)

2 teaspoons salt
1/2 teaspoon freshly ground black pepper
4-pound pullet, disjointed
4 tablespoons butter
3 tablespoons warmed cognac
1/4 cup chopped shallots or green onions
1 cup champagne
1 tomato, peeled and chopped
1/2 teaspoon paprika
1/2 teaspoon tarragon
1 egg yolk
1/4 cup heavy cream

Rub the salt and pepper into the chicken. Melt the butter in a heavy saucepan or Dutch oven; brown the chicken in it. Set the cognac aflame and pour over the chicken. Add the shallots, champagne, tomato, paprika, and tarragon. Cover, and cook over low heat for 1 hour, or until chicken is tender.

Beat together the egg yolk and cream in a bowl. Pour off most of the sauce from the chicken, and gradually add it to the egg-yolk mixture, beating constantly to prevent curdling. Return to chicken. Reheat, but do not allow to boil.

Arrange the chicken on a hot platter. Pour the sauce over it. Serve with boiled potatoes and sautéed mushrooms.

Serve with champagne, a white Burgundy, any dry Italian white wine, or an American white wine.

Serves 4-6

POLLO EN SALSA DE VINO
(chicken in wine sauce)

5-pound roasting chicken, disjointed	1/2 teaspoon thyme
1/3 cup flour	2 tablespoons minced parsley
2 teaspoons salt	1 1/2 cups dry white wine
1/2 teaspoon freshly ground black pepper	2 cups cooked or canned green peas
3 tablespoons olive oil	3 pimientos, cut julienne
1 cup chopped onion	1/2 teaspoon saffron
1 clove garlic, minced	

Wash and dry the chicken pieces; roll in a mixture of the flour, salt, and pepper. Heat the oil in a Dutch oven or deep skillet; add the chicken, onion, and garlic. Cook until chicken is browned. Add the thyme, parsley, and wine. Bring to a boil, cover, and cook over low heat 45 minutes. Add the peas, pimientos, and saffron; cook 10 minutes longer, or until the chicken is tender.

Serve with a white Burgundy or Bordeaux, champagne, a Loire Valley wine like Pouilly-Fumé, an Alsatian wine like Traminer, or an American white or rosé wine.

Serves 4-6

COQ AU VIN BLANC
(chicken in white wine sauce)

2 2 1/2-pound fryers,
    quartered
1/4 cup flour
2 teaspoons salt
1/2 teaspoon freshly
    ground black pepper
1/4 cup olive oil
3/4 cup chopped onion
1/2 cup grated carrot
2 cloves garlic, minced
2 teaspoons finely
    chopped bay leaves

3 tablespoons minced
    parsley
1/4 teaspoon thyme
3 cups dry white wine
1/2 pound mushrooms,
    sliced
3 tablespoons butter
2 cloves
12 small white onions

Wash and dry the chicken. Dip in a mixture of the flour, salt, and pepper. Heat the oil in a deep skillet or casserole; brown the chicken in it. Add the chopped onion, carrot, and garlic; cook 10 minutes, stirring frequently. Add the bay leaves, parsley, thyme, and wine. Bring to a boil, cover, and cook over medium heat 10 minutes.

Sauté the mushrooms in the butter 5 minutes. Stick the cloves in one of the white onions. Add the onions and mushrooms to the pan. Re-cover, and cook over low heat 20 minutes, or until chicken is tender. (If sauce is too thin, thicken with 1 tablespoon flour kneaded with 1 tablespoon butter.)

Serve with a dry white Burgundy or Bordeaux, a dry German white wine, a Loire Valley wine like Pouilly-Fumé, or any American white wine.

Serves 6-8

COQ AU VIN ROUGE
(chicken in red wine)

1/4 pound bacon
6 tablespoons butter
3-pound fryer, disjointed
1 1/2 teaspoons salt
1/4 teaspoons freshly
    ground black pepper
1/4 cup warmed cognac
3 cups dry red wine
1 clove garlic, minced

2 teaspoons tomato paste
1 teaspoon finely chopped
    bay leaf
1/4 teaspoon thyme
12 small white onions
1/2 cup boiling water
12 mushroom caps
1 tablespoon cornstarch
2 tablespoons dry sherry

Cook the bacon in boiling water 10 minutes. Drain and dry. In a casserole or Dutch oven, brown the bacon. Remove bacon, crumble, and set aside; pour off all but 1 tablespoon fat. Add 2 tablespoons butter to the fat; brown the chicken in it. Season with the salt and pepper. Set the cognac aflame, and pour it over the chicken. When flames die, add the wine, garlic, tomato paste, bay leaf, thyme, and bacon bits. Cover, and cook over low heat 30 minutes or until chicken is tender.

While the chicken is cooking, prepare the vegetables. Melt 2 tablespoons butter in a skillet; sauté the onions until browned, shaking the pan frequently. Add the boiling water; cover, and cook over low heat 20 minutes. Season with salt and pepper. Sauté the mushrooms in the remaining butter 5 minutes.

Skim the fat from the chicken gravy. Mix the cornstarch with the sherry; stir into the gravy until thickened. Add the onions and mushrooms, and taste for seasoning. Cover, and cook over low heat 10 minutes.

Serve with a red Bordeaux, a red Burgundy like Beaujolais, an Italian red wine like Valpolicella, or any American red wine.

Serves 4-5

LIQUORED CHICKEN

3 1/2-pound fryer, disjointed
1 1/2 teaspoons salt
1/4 teaspoon white pepper
1/4 pound butter
2 tablespoons olive oil

1/4 cup cognac
1/4 cup bourbon
1/4 cup port or sweet sherry
2 egg yolks
2 cups heavy cream

Rub the chicken pieces with the salt and pepper. Heat 3 tablespoons butter and the olive oil in a skillet; cook the chicken in it until browned and tender. Transfer to a covered hot dish and place in a 325° oven while preparing the sauce.

Drain the fat from the skillet. Into the skillet, stir the cognac, bourbon, and port, scraping the bottom for any browned particles. Cook over low heat until reduced to approximately 1/3 original amount.

Beat the egg yolks with the heavy cream. Place over very low heat until it begins to thicken slightly, stirring steadily. Add the remaining butter. Blend in the liquors, taste for seasoning, and pour over chicken. Do not allow sauce to boil. Serve with rice.

Serve with a white Burgundy, or an American *rosé*.

Serves 4

STUFFED CHICKEN IN SHERRY

1/2 pound chicken livers	3 teaspoons salt
6 tablespoons butter	3/4 teaspoon freshly
1/4 pound ham, cut	ground black pepper
julienne	6-pound roasting chicken
3 pimientos, cut julienne	or capon
2 hard-cooked egg yolks,	1 teaspoon vinegar
chopped	3/4 cup dry sherry
1 teaspoon paprika	

Wash the livers, removing any discolored areas. Cut each liver in quarters. Melt 2 tablespoons butter in a skillet; sauté the livers 5 minutes. Mix in the ham, pimientos, chopped egg yolks, paprika, 1 teaspoon of the salt, and 1/4 teaspoon pepper. Rub the chicken with the remaining salt and pepper; stuff with the liver mixture. Close the opening with skewers, thread, or aluminum foil, and truss.

Melt the remaining butter in a roasting pan; place the chicken in it. Roast in a 375° oven 2 1/4 hours, or until tender, basting occasionally. Transfer the chicken to a heated platter. Place the pan over direct heat and stir in the vinegar and sherry. Bring to a boil, scraping the bottom of any browned particles. Pour over the chicken.

Serve with a red Bordeaux, a dry white Burgundy, an Italian dry white wine like Verdicchio, an Alsatian wine like Riesling, or a *rosé*.

Serves 4-6

BRAISED PULLET IN WINE CREAM

4-pound pullet, disjointed	1/4 teaspoon white
2 tablespoons butter	pepper
1 1/2 teaspoons salt	1/2 cup chopped onion

3/4 cup dry white wine	12 mushroom caps,
2 tablespoons dry sherry	sautéed
1 bay leaf } tied	1/2 cup heavy cream,
3 sprigs parsley } together	scalded
1/4 teaspoon thyme	1 tablespoon lemon juice
	1 truffle, sliced

Wash and dry the chicken pieces. Melt the butter in a deep skillet; add the chicken, salt, pepper, and chopped onion. Cover the pan, and cook over low heat 25 minutes, turning the chicken pieces several times. Add the wine, sherry, bay leaf, parsley, and thyme, and cook 15 minutes longer, or until chicken is tender. Discard bay leaf and parsley. Arrange chicken on a hot serving dish and garnish with mushrooms. Add the cream and lemon juice to the pan juices. Bring to a boil, and strain sauce over the chicken. Garnish with the truffle.

Serve with a dry American or German white wine, a white Bordeaux or Burgundy, a dry Italian white wine, or a rosé.

Serves 4

POLLO AL CAZADOR
(chicken in wine, hunter's style)

2 3-pound fryers, disjointed	1 cup sliced green peppers
1/2 cup flour	1 bay leaf
2 1/2 teaspoons salt	1/2 teaspoon oregano
1/2 teaspoon freshly ground black pepper	1/8 teaspoon dried ground red peppers
1/3 cup olive oil	1 1/2 cups dry red wine
8 small white onions	1 1/2 cups drained canned chick-peas
1 cup peeled, chopped tomatoes	
1/2 cup mushrooms, sliced	

Wash and dry the chicken pieces; roll in a mixture of the flour, salt, and black pepper. Heat the oil in a casserole or Dutch oven; brown the chicken in it. Add the onions, tomatoes, and mushrooms; cook over medium heat 10 minutes, stirring frequently. Add the green peppers, bay leaf, oregano, dried red peppers, wine, and chick-peas. Bring to a boil, cover, and cook over low heat 45 minutes, or until chicken is tender. Taste for seasoning.

Serve with a red Bordeau, a red Burgundy, especially a Beaujolais, a red Italian wine like Bardolino, or any dry American red wine.

Serves 6-8

POULET MARENGO
(chicken marengo)

2 2 1/2-pound broilers, disjointed
1/2 cup flour
2 1/2 teaspoons salt
3/4 teaspoon freshly ground black pepper
2 tablespoons olive oil
2 tablespoons butter
3 cloves garlic
1 cup dry white wine
2 tablespoons cognac
1 cup peeled, diced tomatoes
1 bay leaf
1/4 teaspoon marjoram
1/2 pound mushrooms, quartered
1/4 cup sliced stuffed green olives
2 tablespoons minced parsley

Wash and dry the chicken pieces; toss in a mixture of the flour, salt and pepper. Heat the olive oil and butter in a casserole; brown the chicken in it. Add the garlic, wine, cognac, tomatoes, bay leaf, and marjoram. Bring to a boil, cover, and cook over low heat 25 minutes. Add the mushrooms and olives; cook 10 minutes longer, or until chicken is tender. Taste for seasoning, sprinkle with parsley, and garnish with sautéed French bread slices around the edges.

Serve with a white Burgundy or Bordeaux, a Loire Valley wine like Chinon, or a dry German white or American white wine.

Serves 6-8

POLLO ALLA SICILIANA
(sautéed chicken with eggplant)

3/4 pound small white onions, peeled
3 1/2-pound fryer,
disjointed
2 tablespoons butter
1/3 cup olive oil

2 1/2 teaspoons salt
1/2 teaspoon black
    pepper
1 clove garlic, minced
3/4 cup Marsala or
    sweet sherry

1 cup peeled, diced
    tomatoes
3 tablespoons minced
    parsley
1 small eggplant,
    peeled and sliced
1/3 cup flour

Cook the onions in boiling water 5 minutes; drain and dry. Wash and dry the chicken. Heat the butter and 3 tablespoons of the oil in a skillet; brown the chicken and onions in it. Add 1 1/2 teaspoons of the salt, the pepper, garlic, and wine; cook over medium heat until almost all the wine is evaporated. Mix in the tomatoes and parsley. Cover, and cook over low heat 30 minutes, or until chicken is tender. Taste for seasoning.

While the chicken is cooking, dip the eggplant slices in the flour, then sauté in the remaining oil until browned on both sides. Sprinkle with the remaining salt. Arrange the eggplant slices on a heated platter, with the chicken over it.

Serve with a dry Italian white wine like Soave, a white Burgundy, a dry German or American white wine, or a *rosé*.

Serves 4

POULET À LA NIÇOISE
(chicken with tomatoes and olives)

3 tablespoons olive oil
2 tablespoons butter
5-pound roasting chicken,
    disjointed
2 teaspoons salt
1/2 teaspoon freshly
    ground black pepper
1 teaspoon saffron
3 cloves garlic, minced
1 teaspoon finely crushed
    bay leaves

1/4 teaspoon thyme
2 1/2 cups peeled, diced
    tomatoes
1 1/2 cups dry white
    wine
1 cup water
1/2 cup pitted green
    olives
1/2 cup pitted black
    olives

Heat the olive oil and butter in a casserole; brown the chicken in it. Sprinkle with the salt, pepper, and saffron, and add the garlic, bay leaves, thyme, tomatoes, wine, and water. Bring to a boil, cover, and cook over low heat 1 hour or until chicken is tender. Add the olives. Taste for seasoning, and cook 10 minutes longer.

Serve with a white Burgundy, an Alsatian wine like Riesling, a Loire Valley wine like Pouilly-Fumé, or any American white wine.

Serves 4-6

POLLO EN SALSA DE HUEVOS
(chicken in egg sauce)

2 3-pound fryers, disjointed	1 cup water
2 1/2 teaspoons salt	3 eggs
1/2 teaspoon freshly ground black pepper	3 tablespoons lemon juice
4 tablespoons butter	1 1/2 teaspoons dry mustard
1 1/2 cups dry white wine	1 teaspoon sugar

Wash and dry the chicken; rub with the salt and pepper. Melt the butter in a casserole; brown the chicken in it. Add the wine and water; cover, and cook over low heat 45 minutes or until tender.

Beat the eggs, lemon juice, mustard, and sugar in the top of a double boiler. Place over hot water and cook, stirring steadily until thickened. Add the gravy from the chicken to the mixture, and pour over the chicken. Cook over low heat, basting steadily until chicken is well coated.

Serve with a white Burgundy, a dry American or German white wine, a Loire Valley wine like Sancerre, or a rosé.

Serves 6-8

POULARDE À L'ESTRAGON
(chicken with tarragon)

4-pound pullet	teaspoon dried tarragon
2 teaspoons salt	
1/2 teaspoon freshly ground black pepper	6 tablespoons butter
Bunch of tarragon, or 1 1/2	1/2 cup dry white wine

Clean, wash, and dry the chicken; rub with the salt and pepper. Place 3/4 of the bunch of tarragon or 1 teaspoon dried tarragon in the cavity; truss the chicken.

Melt the butter in a small shallow roasting plan; place the chicken in it. Roast in a 375° oven 1 1/2 hours, or until chicken is tender. Baste frequently. Remove chicken from oven and transfer to a heated platter. Stir the wine and the remaining tarragon into the pan; cook over direct heat, scraping the bottom of the pan, until mixture boils; then cook 2 minutes. Carve the chicken and pour the wine sauce over it.

Serve with a white Burgundy, a dry American or German white wine, or, if you wish, with a *rosé*.

Serves 4-5

POULARDE BASQUAISE
(chicken, basque style)

5-pound roasting chicken, disjointed
2 teaspoons salt
1/2 teaspoon freshly ground black pepper
1/4 cup olive oil
2 tablespoons butter
8 small white onions
1/2 pound mushrooms, sliced
2 cups peeled, diced eggplant
2 cloves garlic, minced
1 cup finely sliced green peppers
3 tomatoes, peeled and quartered
2 teaspoons finely crushed bay leaves
1/2 teaspoon basil
1/2 teaspoon thyme
3/4 cup dry white wine

Rub the chicken pieces with the salt and pepper. Heat the oil in a skillet; brown the chicken in it. Transfer to a casserole. Add the butter to the oil remaining in the skillet, sauté the onions 5 minutes. Mix the mushrooms, eggplant, garlic, green peppers, tomatoes, bay leaves, basil and thyme. Sauté 5 minutes. Spread around the chicken. Stir the wine into the skillet and scrape the bottom of any browned particles; pour over the chicken mixture. Bring to a boil, cover, and bake in a 350° oven 50 minutes, or until chicken is tender. Taste for seasoning.

Serve with a white Burgundy, an Alsatian wine, or a dry American or German white wine.

Serves 4

POLLO PIQUANTE
(chicken in spicy sauce)

2 2 1/2-pound fryers,
    disjointed
2 teaspoons salt
3/4 teaspoon freshly
    ground black pepper
3 tablespoons flour
4 tablespoons olive oil
1 cup chopped onion
1 1/2 cups dry white
    wine
1 tablespoon tomato
    paste

1/2 cup chicken broth
3/4 cup wine vinegar
2 teaspoons anchovy
    paste
2 cloves garlic, minced
1 tablespoon capers
3 tablespoons chopped
    sweet pickles
2 tablespoons chopped
    parsley

Wash and dry the chicken pieces; rub with a mixture of
the salt, pepper, and flour. Heat the oil in a casserole;
sauté the onion 5 minutes. Add the chicken, and cook
until browned. Stir in the wine, tomato paste, and broth.
Cover, and cook over medium heat 45 minutes, or until
chicken is tender.

In a small saucepan, cook the vinegar over high heat
until reduced to half. Add the anchovy paste, garlic, capers,
pickles, and parsley. Cook 1 minute; pour over the chicken
and serve.

Serve with a white American wine, a white Rhône wine
like Hermitage Blanc, a dry Italian white like Orvieto, or
a rosé.

Serves 6-8

POLLO CON PAN
(chicken with bread crumbs)

4-pound roasting chicken,
    disjointed
1/4 cup flour
2 teaspoons salt
1/2 teaspoon freshly
    ground black pepper
4 tablespoons olive oil

1 cup diced onion
2 cloves garlic, minced
1 1/2 cups dry white
    wine
1/2 cup hot chicken broth
1 teaspoon finely chopped
    bay leaf

1/4 teaspoon marjoram
1/4 cup ground almonds
1/2 teaspoon saffron
2 tablespoons butter

1/2 cup fresh fine bread
 crumbs
2 hard-cooked eggs,
 chopped

Wash and dry the chicken; roll in a mixture of the flour, salt, and pepper. Heat the oil in a Dutch oven or deep skillet; lightly brown the chicken in it. Add the onion and garlic; cook 5 minutes. Mix in the wine; cook over high heat 10 minutes. Add the broth, bay leaf, and marjoram. Cover, and cook over low heat 30 minutes. Mix in the almonds and saffron; re-cover, and cook 20 minutes longer, or until chicken is tender.

Melt the butter in a skillet; lightly brown the bread crumbs in it. Sprinkle the chicken with the bread crumbs and chopped eggs just before serving.

Serve with any white American wine, a *rosé*, or any dry Italian white wine like Verdicchio or Soave.

Serves 4

POLLO CON FRUTAS
(chicken with fruit)

2 3-pound fryers,
 disjointed
2 1/2 teaspoons salt
1/2 teaspoon white
 pepper
4 tablespoons butter
1 1/2 cups shredded
 canned pineapple

3/4 cup seedless raisins
1/2 cup ground blanched
 almonds
1 1/2 cups orange juice
1 cup sweet sherry
1/4 teaspoon cinnamon
1/4 teaspoon mace

Wash and dry the chicken pieces; season with the salt and pepper. Melt the butter in a Dutch oven or casserole; brown the chicken in it. Add the pineapple, raisins, almonds, orange juice, sherry, cinnamon, and mace. Bring to a boil, cover, and cook over low heat 45 minutes, or until chicken is tender. Taste for seasoning.

Serve with a light red Bordeaux, a white Burgundy, a dry Italian white wine like Orvieto, or a dry American white wine.

Serves 6-8

POULET EN CASSEROLE
(casserole of chicken)

5-pound roasting chicken, disjointed
2 teaspoons salt
1/2 teaspoon freshly ground black pepper
1 teaspoon paprika
4 tablespoons olive oil
2 tablespoons butter
1/2 cup sliced carrot
3/4 cup diced onion
1 clove garlic, minced
1/2 cup julienne-cut ham
1/2 teaspoon marjoram
1 bay leaf
1 1/4 cups dry white wine
2 tablespoons cognac

Season the chicken pieces with the salt, pepper, and paprika. Heat the oil in a casserole. Brown the chicken pieces in it. Pour off the oil. Add the butter, carrot, onion, garlic, ham, marjoram, and bay leaf. Cook over low heat 5 minutes, stirring frequently. Mix in the wine, cover, and cook 35 minutes over low heat, or until chicken is tender. Season to taste. Warm the cognac and pour over the chicken. Set aflame and serve at once.

Serve with a white Burgundy, a dry American or German white wine, a dry Italian white wine like white Chianti, or a *rosé*.

Serves 4-6

CHICKEN–NOODLE CASSEROLE À LA REINE

6 tablespoons butter
1/2 cup chopped onion
1/4 pound mushrooms, sliced
1/4 cup chopped green pepper
2 tablespoons flour
1 1/2 cups hot chicken broth
1 1/4 cups light cream
2 egg yolks
1 teaspoon salt
1/4 teaspoon freshly ground black pepper
1/2 cup dry sherry
3 cups diced cooked chicken
1/2 pound medium noodles, cooked and drained
1/2 cup grated Parmesan cheese

Melt 4 tablespoons of the butter in a skillet; sauté the onion, mushrooms, and green pepper 5 minutes, stirring frequently. Blend in the flour; add the broth and cream, stirring steadily to the boiling point, then cook over low heat 5 minutes.

Beat the egg yolks in a bowl with the salt, pepper, and sherry; gradually add the hot sauce, stirring steadily to prevent curdling. Mix in the chicken and noodles. Taste for seasoning. Turn into a 3-quart casserole; sprinkle with the cheese and dot with the remaining butter. Bake in a preheated 350° oven 25 minutes, or until top is browned.

Serve with a rather light red Bordeaux, or a German or American white wine.

Serves 4-6

POLLO EN SALSA DE ALMENDRAS
(chicken and almond casserole)

5-pound roasting chicken,
    disjointed
2 teaspoons salt
1/2 teaspoon freshly
    ground black pepper
1/4 cup olive oil
1 cup chopped onion

1 clove garlic, minced
3/4 cup chicken broth
3/4 cup dry sherry
2 tablespoons lemon juice
1 cup finely ground
    blanched almonds

Season the chicken with the salt and pepper. Heat the oil in a casserole; brown the chicken in it. Add the onion and garlic; cook 10 minutes, stirring frequently. Mix in the broth, sherry, and lemon juice. Cover, and cook over low heat 45 minutes. Blend in the almonds. Re-cover, and cook 15 minutes longer, or until chicken is tender.

Serve with a white American wine, a dry Italian white like Verdicchio, a dry German white wine, or a *rosé*.

Serves 6-8

CHICKEN IN ALMOND SAUCE

2 teaspoons salt
1/4 teaspoon freshly
    ground black pepper
2 2 1/2-pound fryers,
    disjointed
1/4 pound butter
3 tablespoons cognac

3 tomatoes, peeled
    and chopped
1 1/2 cups champagne or
    dry white wine
1 cup ground almonds
1/2 cup heavy cream

Sprinkle the salt and pepper on the chicken parts.

Melt the butter (reserving 2 tablespoons) in a heavy

saucepan. Brown the chicken parts in it on both sides. Add the cognac and tomatoes. Cook over medium heat for 5 minutes. Mix in the champagne or white wine and 1/2 cup of the almonds. Cover, and cook over low heat 40 minutes, or until the chicken is tender. Stir in the cream. Taste for seasoning.

Arrange the chicken in a buttered casserole. Pour the sauce over it, and sprinkle with the remaining almonds. Dot with the reserved 2 tablespoons of butter. Bake in a 400° oven for 15 minutes, or until delicately browned on top.

Serve with champagne, a white American wine, or, if you wish, with a *rosé*.

Serves 6-8

FRICASSEE AU VIN BLANC
(French fricassee in white wine)

4-pound pullet, disjointed	1 bay leaf
2 1/2 teaspoons salt	1 clove garlic, minced
1/2 teaspoon freshly ground black pepper	1/4 teaspoon thyme
	2 sprigs parsley
3 tablespoons flour	2 egg yolks
4 tablespoons butter	4 tablespoons heavy cream
1 1/2 cups dry white wine	2 teaspoons lemon juice
1/2 cup chicken broth	

Rub the chicken with the salt, pepper, and flour. Melt the butter in a casserole or Dutch oven, and brown the chicken well. Stir in the wine, broth, bay leaf, garlic, thyme, and parsley. Bring to a boil over direct heat. Cover, and bake in a 350° oven 45 minutes, or until chicken is tender. Remove chicken. Remove bay leaf and parsley and discard.

Beat the egg yolks, cream, and lemon juice in a bowl. Mix in a little of the hot sauce, stirring constantly to prevent curdling. Pour into the casserole, stirring until well mixed. Taste for seasoning. Return the chicken to casserole and reheat, but do not boil.

Serve with a dry American or German white wine, a dry Italian white wine like Soave, or a *rosé*.

Serves 4

ITALIAN CHICKEN FRICASSEE

4-pound pullet, disjointed
1/4 cup flour
1/4 cup olive oil
1 cup chopped onion
1 cup dry white wine
1 clove garlic, minced
2 anchovy fillets, minced
2 tablespoons minced
    capers
1/4 cup ground almonds
1/2 cup chopped parsley
2 teaspoons salt
1/2 teaspoon black
    pepper
1 teaspoon marjoram

Wash and dry the chicken pieces; roll in the flour. Heat the oil in a Dutch oven or heavy saucepan; brown the chicken in it. Remove the chicken, and in the fat remaining, brown the chopped onion. Return the chicken; add the wine, and cook over medium heat 10 minutes. Pound the garlic, anchovies, capers, nuts, parsley, salt, pepper, and marjoram to a paste. Mix into the pan turning the chicken a few times to coat the pieces. Cover, and cook over low heat 45 minutes, or until chicken is tender. If necessary, add small amounts of boiling water from time to time to keep chicken from burning.

Serve with a white Burgundy, a dry Italian white wine like Soave, a dry American or German white wine, or a *rosé*.

Serves 4

POLLO CON PEPERONI
(chicken with peppers)

5-pound roasting chicken,
    disjointed
1/4 cup flour
2 teaspoons salt
1/2 teaspoon freshly
    ground black pepper
4 tablespoons butter
1/2 cup finely chopped
    onion
1/4 cup julienne-cut ham
3/4 cup dry white wine
1/4 teaspoon rosemary
1 cup peeled, chopped
    tomatoes
2 tablespoons olive oil
2 green peppers, cut
    julienne
1 clove garlic, minced

Rub the chicken pieces with a mixture of the flour, salt, and pepper. Melt 2 tablespoons butter in a skillet (with ovenproof handle); brown the chicken in it. Remove. Melt

the remaining butter in the skillet; sauté the onion and
ham 5 minutes. Return the chicken to skillet and add the
wine and rosemary; cook over low heat until wine is absorbed. Add the tomatoes. Cover and bake in a 350° oven
45 minutes.

While the chicken is baking, heat the oil in a skillet;
sauté the green peppers 10 minutes. Add to the chicken,
with the garlic. Re-cover, and bake 15 minutes longer.
Taste for seasoning.

Serve with a dry white Bordeaux or Burgundy, a dry
American or German white wine, an Alsatian white like
Traminer, or a *rosé*.

Serves 4-5

POLLO CON FUNGHI
(chicken and mushrooms)

3 1/2-pound fryer,
    disjointed
1/2 cup flour
2 1/2 teaspoons salt
1/2 teaspoon freshly
    ground black pepper
1/4 cup olive oil
1 clove garlic, minced
1 cup dry white wine

1 cup peeled, diced
    tomatoes
1/4 teaspoon thyme
1/2 pound mushrooms,
    sliced
3 tablespoons butter
2 tablespoons minced
    parsley

Roll the chicken pieces in a mixture of the flour, 2 teaspoons of the salt, and the pepper. Heat the oil in a heavy
skillet; brown the chicken in it. Add the garlic, wine,
tomatoes, and thyme. Cover, and cook over low heat 20
minutes, or until the chicken is tender. While the chicken
is cooking, sauté the mushrooms and remaining salt in the
butter. Add to the chicken just before serving. Sprinkle
with the parsley.

Serve with a white American wine, a dry German white
wine, a dry Italian white wine like Orvieto, or a *rosé*.

Serves 4

CHICKEN WITH MUSHROOMS IN CREAM SAUCE

2 3 1/2-pound fryers,
    disjointed

1/2 cup flour
2 teaspoons salt

1/2 teaspoon freshly
   ground black pepper
6 tablespoons butter
3 tablespoons cognac
1/2 cup chopped onion

1/2 pound mushrooms,
   sliced
2 tablespoons cornstarch
1 cup dry white wine
1/2 cup chicken broth
1/2 cup heavy cream

Wash and dry the chicken pieces; roll in a mixture of the flour, salt, and pepper.

Melt 4 tablespoons butter in a skillet; sauté the chicken until browned on all sides. Transfer chicken to a casserole. Heat the cognac in a ladle; set aflame and pour over the chicken.

Melt the remaining butter in the skillet; sauté the onion and mushrooms 5 minutes. Mix the cornstarch with the wine, then stir into the skillet with the broth. Bring to a boil, stirring constantly. Stir in the cream, then add to the chicken. Cover, and bake in a 350° oven 45 minutes, or until chicken is tender. Taste for seasoning.

Serve with champagne, a dry American or German white wine, or a *rosé*.

Serves 6-8

POULET NIVERNAIS
(chicken with dumplings)

2 3-pound fryers,
   disjointed
4 teaspoons salt
1/2 teaspoon freshly
   ground black pepper
1/4 pound butter
2 cloves
12 small white onions
1 cup sliced mushrooms
1 clove garlic, minced
1/4 teaspoon thyme
1/2 teaspoon marjoram
1 bay leaf

1 1/4 cups dry white
   wine
1/2 teaspoon saffron
1 cup sour cream,
   scalded
1 1/2 cups sifted flour
2 teaspoons baking
   powder
2 eggs, beaten
1/3 cup milk
1 tablespoon minced
   parsley

Season the chicken with 3 teaspoons of the salt, and the pepper. Melt the butter in a casserole or heavy saucepan; brown the chicken in it. Stick the cloves in an onion and add with all the onions and the mushrooms; cook over low heat 5 minutes. Stir in the garlic, thyme, marjoram, bay leaf, and wine. Cover, and bake in a 375° oven 45 minutes, or until chicken is almost tender. Remove from the oven and place over direct low heat. Stir the saffron and sour cream into the pan; taste for seasoning. While the chicken continues to cook, prepare the dumpling batter.

Sift the flour, baking powder, and remaining salt into a bowl. Beat in the eggs and milk. Drop the mixture by the teaspoon around the edge of the casserole. Cover, and cook 15 minutes without raising the cover. When done, sprinkle with the parsley.

Serve with a dry American or German white wine, or a *rosé*.

Serves 8-10

POLLO À LA MANCHEGA
(chicken and vegetable stew)

3 1/2-pound fryer, disjointed
2 tablespoons butter
2 tablespoons olive oil
1 cup chopped onion
2 cloves garlic, minced
2 tablespoons chopped parsley
1 cup grated carrots
3 cups shredded cabbage
2 teaspoons salt
1/2 teaspoon freshly ground black pepper
3/4 cup dry white wine
1/2 cup pitted green olives

Wash and dry the chicken pieces. Heat the butter and oil in a Dutch oven or casserole; brown the chicken in it. Remove chicken. In the fat remaining in the pan, *sauté* the onion, garlic, and parsley for 10 minutes. Return the chicken and add the carrots, cabbage, salt, and pepper. Cook over low heat 10 minutes. Add the wine and olives. Cover, and cook over low heat 45 minutes, or until the chicken is tender.

Serve with a white Burgundy, Bordeaux, a dry American or German white wine, or a *rosé*.

Serves 4

STUFFED BROILERS

2 2 1/2-pound broilers,
   split
3 teaspoons salt
3/4 teaspoon freshly
   ground black pepper
6 slices white bread,
   trimmed
3/4 pound chicken livers

6 tablespoons butter
1 cup chopped onion
1/2 cup chopped celery
   and leaves
1/4 teaspoon thyme
2 tablespoons minced
   parsley
1/2 cup dry sherry

Wash and dry the chicken halves; season with 2 teaspoons
salt and 1/2 teaspoon pepper. Soak the bread in water,
then drain and mash. Chop the raw livers.

Melt 3 tablespoons of the butter in a skillet; sauté the
onion and celery 5 minutes. Mix in the livers, and the remaining salt and pepper; sauté 5 minutes, stirring frequently. Mix in the bread, thyme, and parsley; taste for
seasoning.

Melt the remaining butter in a baking pan. Arrange the
chicken halves in it, skin side up. Bake in a 350° oven 20
minutes. Turn over, skin side down, and fill the cavities
with the stuffing. Pour the sherry over the stuffing and
around the chicken. Bake 20 minutes longer, or until the
chicken is tender.

Serve with a white Burgundy or Bordeaux, a Loire Valley wine like Pouilly-Fumé, a dry Italian white wine like
Soave, or a dry white American wine.

Serves 4-8

PUCHERO DE GALLINA
(stuffed poached chicken)

5-pound pullet
3 extra chicken livers
3 teaspoons salt
3/4 teaspoon freshly
   ground black pepper
1 1/2 cups dry bread
   crumbs
1 clove garlic, minced
2 tablespoons chopped
   parsley
1/4 teaspoon thyme

1/4 cup melted butter
2 eggs, beaten
2 cups dry white wine
4 cups water
1 onion
1 carrot
1 parsnip
3 whole cloves garlic
1 tablespoon olive oil
1 tablespoon flour

Wash and dry the chicken. Reserve the livers. Season the chicken with 2 1/2 teaspoons of the salt and 1/2 teaspoon pepper.

Mix together the bread crumbs, garlic, parsley, thyme, butter, and remaining salt and pepper; mix in the eggs. Stuff the chicken, and sew or skewer the opening securely. Truss the chicken.

Combine the wine, water, onion, carrot, parsnip, and garlic in a heavy deep pan. Bring to a boil. Add the chicken; cover, and cook over medium heat 2 1/2 hours, or until the chicken is tender. Remove the chicken to a hot platter and keep hot. Reduce the broth to 2 1/2 cups. Strain.

While the chicken is cooking, chop the livers very fine, then sauté in the oil for 2 minutes. Blend in the flour. Mix a little hot broth with the livers, then combine the mixture with the broth in the pan; cook 5 minutes. Carve the chicken, and pour the sauce over it.

Serve with a white American wine, a dry Italian white wine like Orvieto, or a *rosé*.

Serves 4-6

BREAST OF CHICKEN AND HAM

3 whole chicken breasts	4 tablespoons butter
1/4 cup flour	1/2 teaspoon sage
1 1/2 teaspoons salt	6 slices prosciutto or
1/4 teaspoon white	cooked ham
pepper	3/4 cup dry white wine

Have the chicken breasts cut in half through the breast-bone. Remove the skin and bones. Place each piece of chicken between 2 sheets of waxed paper and pound very thin. Dip the pounded chicken in a mixture of the flour, salt, and pepper.

Melt the butter in a skillet; sauté the chicken breasts until browned on the under side. Turn chicken over and sprinkle with the sage. Cover with the ham. Sauté 5 minutes. Add the wine; bring to a boil, and cook over low heat 2 minutes. Transfer chicken to a heated serving dish, ham side up. Boil the pan juices for 2 minutes, and stir to break up the glaze. Pour over the chicken.

Serve with a white Burgundy, an Alsatian wine like Traminer, a dry American white wine, or a *rosé*.

Serves 6

CHICKEN, CHEESE, AND HAM ROLLS

3 whole chicken breasts	6 thin slices Swiss cheese
1/4 cup flour	6 cooked asparagus tips
2 teaspoons salt	6 tablespoons butter
1/4 teaspoon white	3/4 cup Marsala or sweet
pepper	sherry
6 thin slices cooked ham	

Have the chicken breasts cut in half through the breast-bone. Remove the skin and bones. Place each piece of chicken between two pieces of waxed paper and pound as thin as possible. Dip one side of each piece in a mixture of the flour, salt, and pepper. On the undipped side place a slice of ham, then a slice of cheese and an asparagus tip. Roll up carefully and tie with thread or fasten with tooth-picks.

Melt 4 tablespoons butter in a skillet; sauté the rolls over very low heat until browned and tender. Transfer to a heated serving dish. To the skillet, add the wine and remaining butter. Bring to a boil, scraping the pan for browned particles. Pour over the rolls.

Serve with a red American wine, a red Bordeaux or Burgundy, an Italian red wine like Volpolicella, or a *rosé*.

Serves 6

CHICKENBURGER

2 whole chicken breasts	1 1/4 teaspoons salt
1 pound veal	1/4 teaspoon nutmeg
3 slices white bread,	1/3 cup dry sherry
trimmed	1 cup light cream
3/4 cup milk	4 tablespoons butter

Remove the skin and bones of the chicken; cut the chicken into strips. Cut the veal into small pieces. Grind the veal and chicken in a meat grinder, using the finest blade.

Soak the bread in the milk, mash and squeeze dry. Mix

together the bread, ground meat, salt, nutmeg, sherry, and cream! form into 8–10 flat patties.

Melt the butter in a skillet; sauté the patties in it 10 minutes on each side, or until browned on both sides. Serve with a mushroom or cream sauce, if desired.

Serves 4-5

POULET FINANCIÈRE
(chicken with chicken livers and olives)

4-pound pullet, disjointed
1 1/2 teaspoons salt
1/2 teaspoon freshly
    ground black pepper
1/3 cup flour
2 tablespoons olive oil
1/4 pound mushrooms,
    sliced

1/2 cup chicken broth
1 cup dry red wine
1/2 pound chicken livers,
    cut in halves
4 tablespoons butter
1 tablespoon flour
1/2 cup pitted green
    olives

Wash and dry the chicken pieces; roll in a mixture of the salt, pepper, and flour. Heat the oil in a casserole; brown the chicken in it. Add the mushrooms, chicken broth, and wine. Cover, and cook over low heat 25 minutes. Sauté the livers in 2 tablespoons of the butter. Knead the flour with the remaining butter; add to the gravy in small bits, then add the olives and sautéed livers; cook 10 minutes longer, or until chicken is tender. Taste for seasoning.

Serve with a light red Bordeaux or Burgundy, an Italian red wine like Valpolicella, or a red American wine.

Serves 6-8

SPEZZATO DI POLLO
(chicken and livers in white wine)

2 2 1/2-pound fryers
3 tablespoons olive oil
4 tablespoons butter
2 1/2 teaspoons salt
3/4 teaspoon freshly
    ground black pepper
1 clove garlic, minced
2 tablespoons chopped
    chives or green
    onions

3/4 cup diced
    mushrooms
1 1/2 cups dry white
    wine
1/2 cup chicken broth
1/2 pound chicken livers,
    cut in half
2 tablespoons minced
    parsley

Have the chicken chopped up, bone and all, in small pieces. Wash and dry thoroughly. Heat the oil and 1 tablespoon of the butter in a deep skillet; sauté the chicken in it until browned. Mix in 2 teaspoons of the salt, 1/2 teaspoon pepper, the garlic, chives, mushrooms, wine, and broth. Bring to a boil, and cook over medium heat 30 minutes, or until chicken is tender.

Melt the remaining butter in a separate skillet; sauté the livers in it 5 minutes, or until very little pink remains. Season with the remaining salt and pepper. Add to the chicken; cook 5 minutes longer. Sprinkle with the parsley.

Serve with a dry Italian white wine like Orvieto, a dry white Burgundy or Bordeaux, or a dry American wine.

Serves 6-8

RICE WITH CHICKEN LIVERS AND MUSHROOM SAUCE

6 tablespoons butter	1/4 pound chicken livers, diced
3/4 cup finely chopped onion	1/2 pound mushrooms, sliced
2 cups raw rice	
3/4 cup Marsala or sweet sherry	1/2 cup beef broth
5 cups hot chicken broth	1/4 teaspoon freshly ground black pepper
1 1/2 teaspoons salt	1 bay leaf
1/2 cup thinly sliced onion	1/4 teaspoon thyme
1/2 cup julienne-cut prosciutto ham	

Melt half the butter in a saucepan; sauté the chopped onion until yellow and transparent. Stir in the rice until lightly browned. Add 1/4 cup wine; cook until wine is absorbed. Add 2 cups of the chicken broth and half the salt; cover, and cook over low heat 25 minutes, adding the remaining chicken broth as it becomes absorbed by the rice. Meanwhile prepare the sauce.

Melt the remaining butter in a small saucepan; sauté the sliced onion and ham 5 minutes. Add the livers and mushrooms; sauté 5 minutes, stirring frequently. Mix in the beef broth, pepper, bay leaf, thyme, and the remaining wine and salt. Cook over low heat 10 minutes. Taste for seasoning, and discard the bay leaf. Mix half the sauce with the rice. Heap in a bowl and pour remaining sauce over the top.

Serve with a light American red wine, or a light red Bordeaux or Burgundy.

Serves 4-6

GALLINA CON ARROZ
(chicken in rice ring)

2 3-pound fryers, disjointed	2 1/2 teaspoons salt
3 tablespoons olive oil	1/4 teaspoon dried ground red peppers
1 cup minced onion	1/2 cup seedless raisins
3/4 cup chopped green peppers	4 cups cooked, drained rice
2 cloves garlic, minced	4 tablespoons melted butter
1 tablespoon minced parsley	2 cups grated Cheddar cheese
1 8-ounce can tomato sauce	4 eggs, beaten
2 cups dry white wine	1 cup sliced toasted almonds
1 cup boiling water	

Wash and dry the chicken pieces.

Heat the oil in a Dutch oven or heavy saucepan; sauté the onion and green peppers 5 minutes. Add the garlic, parsley, and chicken; sauté 15 minutes, turning the chicken to brown all sides. Mix in the tomato sauce, wine, water, salt, and ground red peppers. Cover, and cook over low heat for 1 hour, or until chicken is tender. Cut the chicken from the bones and return to the sauce. Add the raisins; cook over low heat 15 minutes. Taste for seasoning.

Mix together the rice, butter, cheese, and eggs. Pack into a 9-inch buttered ring mold. Bake in a 350° oven 20 minutes or until set. Run a knife around the edges and carefully turn out onto a hot platter. Put the chicken mixture in the center and sprinkle with the almonds.

Serve with a dry American or German white wine, a white Burgundy, an Alsatian wine like Traminer, or a *rosé*.

Serves 6-8

SQUABS WITH PEAS

4 squabs
1 tablespoon salt
3/4 teaspoon freshly
    ground black pepper
1/2 teaspoon thyme
4 tablespoons butter
1 1/2 cups chopped
    onion

1/4 pound ham, julienne-
    cut
1 cup dry white wine
1/2 cup chicken broth
1 pound green peas,
    shelled, or 1 package
    frozen peas, thawed

Wash and dry, the squabs; rub inside and out with a mixture of the salt, pepper, and thyme. Melt the butter in a Dutch oven or heavy deep skillet; sauté the chopped onion 10 minutes. Add the squabs; brown on all sides. Mix in the ham and half the wine; cook over medium heat 10 minutes. Mix in the broth and remaining wine; cover, and cook over low heat 30 minutes. Add the peas; re-cover, and cook 15 minutes. Taste for seasoning. Transfer the squabs to a serving dish and pour gravy over all.

Serve with a white Burgundy, a dry German or American white wine, or a *rosé*.

Serves 4

STUFFED SQUABS

1 cup wild rice, washed
    and drained
3 cups chicken broth
1/4 pound butter
1 cup chopped onion
1/4 pound mushrooms,
    chopped
1 teaspoon Worcestershire
    sauce

3/4 teaspoon freshly
    ground black pepper
6 squabs or Rock Cornish
    hens
1 tablespoon salt
1 teaspoon paprika
12 small white onions
1 cup dry white wine
1/4 cup cognac

Combine the wild rice and broth in a saucepan. Cover, bring to a boil, and cook over low heat 25 minutes, or until rice is tender and dry. Melt 4 tablespoons butter in a skillet; sauté the chopped onion and mushrooms 10 minutes. Add to the rice, with the Worcestershire sauce and 1/4 teaspoon pepper. Mix lightly and taste for seasoning.

Season the birds with the salt, paprika, and remaining pepper; stuff, and sew or skewer openings.

Melt the remaining butter in a shallow roasting pan. Brown the birds and whole onions. Add the wine; bake in a 375° oven 40 minutes, or until birds are tender, basting frequently. Remove from oven and pour warmed cognac over the birds. Set aflame, and serve when flames die.

Serve with a white Burgundy, a dry American or German white wine, or a *rosé*.

Serves 6

SQUABS IN RED WINE

4 1-pound squabs	2 tablespoons olive oil
2 teaspoons salt	1 1/2 cups sliced onion
1/2 teaspoon freshly ground black pepper	2 cloves garlic, minced
	2 carrots, sliced
4 slices bacon	2 cups dry red wine

Wash, clean, and dry the squabs. Rub with the salt and pepper. Cut the livers and gizzards in small pieces. Wrap a slice of bacon around each squab and fasten with a toothpick.

Heat the oil in a Dutch oven. Add the squabs, onion slices, garlic and carrots. Cook until squabs are browned on all sides. Add the livers and giblets and wine. Bring to a boil, cover, and cook over low heat 1 hour, or until the squabs are tender. If gravy is too thin, thicken with 1 tablespoon flour kneaded with 1 tablespoon butter.

Serve with a red Bordeaux wine, a Beaujolais, or an American red wine.

Serves 4

CORNISH HEN IN CHERRY SAUCE

2 Rock Cornish hens	1/4 pound (1 stick) butter
2 teaspoons salt	3 tablespoons wine vinegar
1/2 teaspoon freshly ground black pepper	3 tablespoons sugar

| 1 cup port wine | 1 1/2 cups canned pitted |
| 2 teaspoons cornstarch | black cherries |

Season the hens with the salt and pepper. Melt half the butter in a shallow baking pan, and pour into the hens. Bake in a 375° oven 50 minutes, or until birds are browned and tender, basting frequently. Cut birds in half, arrange in a serving platter, and keep warm while making sauce.

Cook the vinegar and sugar until caramel-colored. Add the port wine to the pan juices and reduce to half over high heat, scraping up the glaze from the pan. Stir in the caramel. Mix the cornstarch with 2 tablespoons cold water and stir into the pan, cooking until thickened. Mix in the cherries and the remaining butter, and cook over low heat 5 minutes. Pour sauce over birds and serve, accompanied by wild rice.

Serve with a red Burgundy or Bordeaux, a red Rhône wine like Hermitage or Châteauneuf-du-Pape, or a red American wine.

Serves 2-4

ROCK CORNISH HEN IN CAPER SAUCE

2 Rock Cornish hens, halved	1 tablespoon flour
1 1/2 teaspoons salt	3/4 cup dry white wine
1/2 teaspoon freshly ground black pepper	4 anchovy fillets, mashed
3 tablespoons butter	2 tablespoons drained capers
	2 tablespoons lemon juice

Wash and dry the hens. Season with the salt and pepper. Melt half the butter in a deep skillet. Brown the birds in it very well. Blend in the flour until browned. Add the wine, anchovies, capers, and lemon juice. Cover, and cook over low heat 30 minutes, or until birds are tender. Add the remaining butter.

Serve with a white Burgundy, a dry American or German white wine, or a white Rhône wine like Châteauneuf-du-Pape Blanc, or a rosé.

Serves 2-4

CHAPON SAUTÉ À LA BORDELAISE
(capon, Bordeaux style)

1/4 pound butter	1/2 cup milk
3 tablespoons olive oil	1/2 cup flour
5-pound capon, disjointed	Vegetable oil for deep
2 teaspoons salt	frying
1/2 teaspoon freshly	1 clove garlic, minced
ground black pepper	1 cup dry white wine
1 package frozen	1 teaspoon meat glaze
artichokes, thawed	1 tablespoon tomato
3 potatoes, peeled and	paste
very thinly sliced	
3 large onions, thinly	
sliced	

Heat 2 tablespoons butter and the oil in a heavy sauce-pan; sauté the capon in it until browned on all sides. Season with the salt and pepper. Cover, and cook over low heat 45 minutes, or until the capon is tender. Transfer to a hot serving platter and keep warm.

While chicken is cooking, sauté the artichokes in 3 table-spoons butter for 5 minutes, turning them frequently. Sprinkle with salt. Dry potato slices thoroughly, and sauté in the remaining butter until golden brown on both sides. Sprinkle with salt.

Separate the onion slices into rings. Dip in the milk and then in the flour, and fry in 375° oil until crisp and golden.

Add the garlic to butter remaining in pan in which capon was cooked. Sauté 2 minutes. Add wine, meat glaze, and tomato paste and stir to scrape any browned particles from pan. Cook over low heat 5 minutes.

Arrange the artichokes, potato slices and onion rings around the capon. Pour sauce over capon and serve.

Serve with a white Burgundy, a dry American or German white wine, a white Rhône wine like Hermitage Blanc, or a *rosé*.

Serves 4-6

CHAPON LUCULLUS
(capon in wine sauce)

2 pair sweetbreads	5-pound capon, disjointed
6 tablespoons butter	1 cup sliced onion

1/2 cup sliced carrot
2 teaspoons salt
1/2 teaspoon freshly
    ground black pepper
1 cup sliced mushrooms

1/2 cup diced ham
1 cup dry white wine
1/4 cup cognac
3/4 cup heavy cream

Soak the sweetbreads for 2 hours in cold water to cover. Drain. Cook in lightly salted water 10 minutes. Drain, cool, remove membranes, and dice. Refrigerate while preparing the capon.

Melt half the butter in a casserole. Add the capon pieces, sliced onion, carrots, salt, and pepper. Cover, and cook over low heat 45 minutes, turning the pieces frequently. Add the remaining butter, the mushrooms, ham, sweetbreads, and wine. Cook 20 minutes. Mix in the cognac and cream. Cook 5 minutes. Taste for seasoning.

Serve with a white Burgundy, a Loire Valley wine like Sancerre, a dry Italian white wine like Soave, or a rosé.

Serves 6-8

MARINATED STUFFED TURKEY

12-pound turkey
3 cups dry red wine
2 1/2 chopped onion
2 cloves garlic, minced
5 teaspoons salt
1 teaspoon freshly
    ground black pepper
1 bay leaf
1/3 cup olive oil
3/4 cup chopped green
    peppers

1/2 pound ground pork
2 cups ground almonds
3 hard-cooked eggs
1 1/4 cups seedless
    raisins
1 cup sliced pimiento-
    stuffed green olives
1/2 teaspoon marjoram
1 1/2 cups finely diced
    bread

Wash, clean, and dry the turkey.

In a glass or pottery bowl, combine the wine, 1 cup of the chopped onion, the garlic, 3 teaspoons salt, the pepper, and bay leaf. Marinate the turkey in the mixture in the refrigerator overnight. Turn and baste turkey a few times.

Heat the oil in a skillet; sauté the green peppers and remaining onion 5 minutes. Add the pork, and cook until browned and no pink remains. Season with the remaining salt and mix in the almonds, eggs, raisins, olives, marjoram, and bread. Taste for seasoning. Drain the turkey, stuff, and close the openings with skewers or thread. Place in a roasting pan; roast in a 325° oven for 3 1/2 hours, adding the marinade after 1 hour. Baste frequently until turkey is tender.

Serve with a light red Burgundy, especially a Beaujolais, a Rhône wine like Côte-Rôtie, a dry Italian red wine like Barolo, or an American red wine.

Serves 10-14

CANARD AU GRAND MARNIER
(duck with Grand Marnier)

5-pound duck
2 1/2 teaspoons salt
1 orange, cut in half
1 1/2 cups dry white wine
1/2 cup sugar
3 tablespoons wine
    vinegar

3/4 cup orange juice
1/2 cup Grand Marnier
3 tablespoons grated
    orange rind

Clean the duck, wash, and dry. Rub the salt into the skin and cavity; put the orange in the cavity. Place the duck on a rack in a shallow roasting pan. Roast in a 425° oven 45 minutes, turning the duck to brown all sides. Pour off the fat, remove the rack, and add the wine. Reduce heat to 350°, and roast 1 1/4 hours longer or until the duck is tender. Baste occasionally.

While the duck is roasting, prepare the sauce. Combine the sugar and vinegar in a heavy saucepan; cook over medium heat until caramel-colored. Stir in the orange juice, Grand Marnier, and orange rind. Cook over low heat 5 minutes. Skim the fat from the pan juices and add juices to the sauce. Taste for seasoning.

Carve the duck and pour sauce over it. If desired, warmed cognac may be set aflame on the duck just before serving.

Serve with a red or white Burgundy, or a dry red American wine.

Serves 4

CANARD AU VIN ROUGE
(duck in red wine)

5-pound duck	1 tablespoon chopped onion
2 teaspoons salt	
1/2 teaspoon freshly ground pepper	1 teaspoon chopped parsley
3 tablespoons butter	2 teaspoons grated orange rind
3 tablespoons flour	
1 cup chicken stock	1/4 teaspoon rosemary
1 cup dry red wine	1 bay leaf

Wash the duck, dry, and season with the salt and pepper. Chop the liver and refrigerate. Place the duck on a rack in a shallow pan; roast in a 375° oven 1 1/2 hours, turning the duck to brown all sides. Carve the duck into serving-size pieces, removing as many bones as possible.

Melt the butter in a saucepan; mix in the flour until browned. Add stock and wine, stirring steadily to the boiling point. Add the carved duck, the onion, parsley, orange rind, rosemary, and bay leaf. Cook over low heat 1 hour. Discard the bay leaf. Stir the chopped liver into the sauce; cook 5 minutes. Serve on rounds of toasted bread.

Serve with a red Bordeaux or Burgundy, or a dry red American wine.

Serves 4-5

DUCK AND VEGETABLES IN RED WINE

5-pound duck, disjointed	2 cups dry red wine
1 tablespoon vegetable oil	1/2 cup chicken broth
12 small white onions	1/2 pound mushrooms, sliced
1 carrot, sliced	
1 clove garlic, minced	2 cups cubed sweet potatoes
2 teaspoons salt	
1/2 teaspoon freshly ground black pepper	

Wash the duck pieces, remove as much fat as possible, and dry. Heat the oil in a casserole; brown the duck in it on all sides. Pour off the fat. Add the onions, carrot, garlic, salt, and pepper; cook until onions turn golden. Pour off the fat again. Add the wine and broth. Cover, and cook over low heat 45 minutes. Skim the fat, then add the mushrooms and potatoes. Cook 25 minutes longer. Taste for seasoning.

Serve with a red Burgundy, a Rhône wine like Hermitage, an Italian red wine like Barolo, or a dry red American wine.

Serves 4

CANARD AUX OLIVES
(duck with olives)

5-pound duck	1/2 teaspoon thyme
2 teaspoons salt	1 bay leaf
1/2 teaspoon freshly ground black pepper	1 tablespoon flour
	3/4 cup chicken broth
1 teaspoon paprika	1 1/2 cups sliced stuffed olives
1 cup dry white wine	

Clean the duck, removing as much fat as possible. Season with the salt, pepper, and paprika. Place on a rack in a shallow roasting pan. Roast in a 425° oven 45 minutes, turning the duck to brown all sides. Pour off the fat, remove the rack, and add the wine, thyme, and bay leaf. Reduce heat to 350°, and roast duck 1 hour longer, or until tender, basting frequently.

Transfer the duck to a platter; place pan over direct low heat. Mix the flour with the broth and add to the pan juices, stirring steadily to the boiling point. Add the olives. Cook over low heat 5 minutes. Taste for seasoning. Carve the duck and pour the sauce over it.

Serve with a red Burgundy, a Rhône wine like Châteauneuf-du-Pape, or a dry red American wine.

Serves 4

BRAISED DUCK WITH OLIVE SAUCE

5-6 pound duck, disjointed	1/2 cup diced celery
2 teaspoons salt	1 cup dry red wine
1/2 teaspoon black pepper	1/2 cup beef broth
1/2 teaspoon oregano	1 bay leaf
3/4 cup chopped onion	1 cup sliced black olives

Wash the duck, remove as much fat as possible, and dry, Rub the pieces with a mixture of the salt, pepper, and oregano. In a Dutch oven or heavy casserole, brown the duck pieces on all sides. Pour off the fat. Add the chopped onion and the celery; cook 10 minutes. Pour off the fat again. Add the wine, broth, and bay leaf; bring to a boil, cover, and cook over low heat 1 hour, or until tender. Turn pieces and baste frequently. Arrange the duck on a heated serving dish and keep warm.

Skim the fat off the gravy and discard the bay leaf. Add the olives; cook 5 minutes. Taste for seasoning. Pour the sauce over the duck.

Serve with a dry red Bordeaux or Burgundy, or a dry red American wine.

Serves 4

DUCKLING WITH SOUR RED CHERRIES

5-pound duck	1/2 cup sweet sherry
2 teaspoons salt	2 tablespoons butter
1/2 teaspoon freshly	2 tablespoons flour
ground black pepper	2 cups canned, pitted
1/4 teaspoon marjoram	sour red cherries
2 cups chicken broth	

Wash and dry the duck; rub inside and out with salt, pepper, and marjoram. Combine in a heavy saucepan with the chicken broth. Cover, and cook over low heat for 1 hour, or until duck is tender.

Add the sherry. Cook over high heat 5 minutes. Remove the duck from the gravy, then remove the skin. Carve into serving-size pieces. Place on a hot serving platter and keep hot in the oven. Skim the fat off the gravy.

Knead together the flour and butter. Add to the gravy in small bits, stirring constantly until gravy is thickened. Add the cherries to gravy and pour over the duck. Serve very hot.

Serve with a red Burgundy wine, or a dry red American wine.

Serves 4

CANARD VÉRONIQUE
(braised duck with grapes)

5-pound duck, disjointed	1 cup port wine
1 1/2 teaspoons salt	2 tablespoons currant
1/4 teaspoon freshly	jelly
ground black pepper	1 cup seedless grapes,
1/4 teaspoon nutmeg	cut in half
2 tablespoons butter	

Wash and dry the duck pieces; remove as much fat as possible, then rub with the salt, pepper, and nutmeg.

Melt the butter in a casserole; brown the duck in it. Pour off the fat, and add the port and jelly. Bring to a boil, cover, and cook over low heat 45 minutes, or until duck is tender. Skim off the fat, and add the grapes; cook 5 minutes longer.

Serve with a red Burgundy wine, or a dry red American wine.

Serves 4

ROAST LONG ISLAND DUCK

2 5-pound ducks	1 cup dry sherry
3 teaspoons salt	2 tablespoons cornstarch
1/2 teaspoon pepper	1 cup water
1 cup sugar	3 tablespoons julienne-cut
2 cups currant jelly	orange rind
1 1/2 cups orange juice	

Clean the ducks, and remove as much fat as possible. Season with the salt and pepper. Place on a rack in a roasting pan; roast in a 400° oven 1 1/4 hours, basting frequently. Reduce heat to 350° and roast 1 hour longer, or until the ducks are tender, crisp, and brown.

In a saucepan, combine the sugar, currant jelly, and orange juice. Bring to a boil, and cook over low heat 15 minutes. Stir in the sherry, and cook 5 minutes longer. Mix the cornstarch with the water and add to the saucepan, stirring constantly to the boiling point. Add the rind.

Carve the duck in quarters, and pour the sauce over it. Garnish with a slice of orange and maraschino cherry.

Serve with a dry red American wine.

Serves 6-8

ANITRA ARROSTITA
(roast stuffed duck)

5-6 pound duck
2 teaspoons salt
1/2 teaspoon freshly
    ground black pepper
2 cloves garlic, minced
2 tablespoons olive oil
3/4 cup minced onion
1 pound sausage meat

3 slices toast, diced
1/8 teaspoon crushed
    dried red peppers
1/2 teaspoon rosemary
1/2 cup chopped black
    olives
3/4 cup Marsala wine or
    sweet sherry

Wash and dry the duck; rub inside and out with the salt, pepper, and garlic.

Heat the oil in a skillet; sauté the onion 5 minutes. Add the sausage meat; let brown, stirring frequently, Pour off the fat. Mix in the diced toast, red peppers, rosemary, and olives. Cool 15 minutes. Stuff the duck. Close the opening with skewers, or sew it. Place on a rack in a roasting pan. Roast in a 425° oven 30 minutes. Pour off the fat. Reduce heat to 350°. Roast 30 minutes. Pour off the fat. Remove the rack. Add the wine; roast 1 1/2 hours longer, or until duck is tender, basting frequently.

Serve with a dry red Bordeaux or Burgundy or dry red American wine.

Serves 4-5

DUCK CASSEROLE

5-pound duck, disjointed
1 1/2 teaspoons salt
1/2 teaspoon freshly
    ground black pepper
2 tablespoons vegetable
    oil
3/4 cup chopped onion
1 cup chopped green
    peppers
1 clove garlic, minced

1/2 cup canned tomato
    sauce
1 cup dry sherry
1 bay leaf
1 cup cooked or canned
    green peas
1/2 pound mushrooms,
    sliced and sautéed
1/2 cup sliced pimiento-
    stuffed olives

Wash and dry the duck; remove as much fat as possible. Rub the pieces with the salt and pepper.

Heat the oil in a skillet; brown the duck pieces in it. Drain and transfer to a casserole. In the fat remaining, sauté the chopped onion, green pepper, and garlic 10 minutes. Drain off the fat, and add the vegetables to casserole with the tomato sauce, sherry, and bay leaf. Cover and bake in a 350° oven 1 hour, or until duck is tender. Skim off the fat, discard the bay leaf, and add the peas, mushrooms, and olives. Bake 5 minutes longer.

Serve with a red Burgundy wine or a dry red American wine.

Serves 4

ENTRECÔTE GRILLÉ CHAROLLAIS BOURGUIGNONNE
(grilled steak, Burgundy style)

2 tablespoons butter
2 tablespoons finely
    chopped shallots or
    onion
1/2 teaspoon flour
1 cup dry red wine

1 clove garlic, minced
1 tablespoon tomato paste
1 tablespoon Madeira or
    sweet sherry
1 shell or club steak, cut
    2 inches thick

Melt the butter in a skillet and sauté the shallots until soft but not brown. Blend in the flour. Add the wine, stirring constantly to the boiling point. Mix in the garlic, tomato paste, and Madeira. Cook over low heat 30 minutes.

Broil the steak in a hot broiler to desired degree of rareness. Serve with the red wine sauce.

Serve with a red Burgundy or Bordeaux, a red Rhône wine like Châteauneuf-du-Pape, an Italian red wine like Barolo, or an American red wine.

Serves 2

STEAK AU POIVRE
(pepper steak)

1 tablespoon black
    peppercorns
2 boneless club or shell
    steaks, cut 1 inch
    thick
1 tablespoon olive oil
2 tablespoons sweet
    butter

1 tablespoon chopped
    shallots or onion
1 cup dry red wine
1 teaspoon prepared
    French mustard
1 teaspoon Worcestershire
    sauce

Crush the peppercorns coarsely. (Put them in a towel and pound with a hammer, or use a mortar and pestle, or put through a coarse peppermill.) With the heel of the hand, press the crushed peppercorns well into both sides of the steaks.

Heat the oil in a skillet; quickly brown the steaks in it
on both sides. While the steaks are browning, melt 1 tablespoon butter in another skillet; sauté the chopped shallots
2 minutes. Then add the steaks, and cook 2 minutes on
each side. Remove the steaks to a heated platter and keep
hot. Add the wine to the shallots; cook over high heat
until reduced to 1/4 the original quantity. Remove from
the heat and immediately stir in the mustard, Worcestershire sauce, and the remaining butter, broken into small
pieces. Pour over the steaks.

Serve with a red Burgundy or Bordeaux, a dry Italian
red wine, or an American red wine.

Serves 2-4

BOEUF RÔTI À LA BORDELAISE
(roast beef, Bordeaux style)

3-pound rump roast of beef	1/2 cup olive oil
1 onion, sliced	1 cup dry white wine
2 shallots, chopped	2 teaspoons salt
4 sprigs parsley	1/2 teaspoon freshly ground black pepper
1 bay leaf	1 tablespoon wine vinegar
1/2 teaspoon thyme	

Trim the fat from meat and reserve. Marinate the meat
overnight in a mixture of the sliced onion, shallots, parsley,
bay leaf, thyme, oil, wine, salt, and pepper.

Put a strip of the reserved beef fat in the bottom of a
roasting pan. Strain the marinade and spread the vegetables and herbs on the fat. Put meat on top and season
with salt and pepper; place another piece of fat over it and
add 1/4 cup marinade. Roast in a 350° oven 1 1/4 hours,
basting often. Transfer meat to a serving platter and keep
hot.

Strain juices from roasting pan; skim off the fat, and
combine the juice in a saucepan with the remaining
strained marinade. Cook over high heat 10 minutes. Add
wine vinegar, reheat, and serve separately as a sauce for
roast.

Serve with a dry red Bordeaux or Burgundy, or a dry red American wine.

Serves 6-8

CARNE ASADO
(marinated roast beef)

6-pound rolled roast of beef
2 teaspoons salt
1 teaspoon freshly ground black pepper
1 teaspoon Spanish paprika
3 cloves garlic, minced
1 1/2 cups dry red wine
1/2 cup wine vinegar
1/4 cup olive oil

2 cups chopped onion
1 cup chopped green peppers
2 cups peeled diced tomatoes
1 bay leaf
1 cup sliced sautéed mushrooms
1 8-ounce can green peas, drained

Rub the meat with a mixture of the salt, pepper, paprika, and garlic. Marinate the meat in a mixture of the wine and vinegar in the refrigerator 24 hours, turning the meat and basting a few times. Remove from refrigerator 2 hours before roasting.

Drain the meat, reserving the marinade. Heat the oil in a roasting pan over direct heat; brown the meat in it on all sides. Pour off half the fat. Add the chopped onion, green peppers, tomatoes, bay leaf, and half the marinade. Insert a meat thermometer in the center of the meat and roast in a 350° oven to desired degree of rareness, basting frequently (or without thermometer about 13 minutes per pound for rare, 15 for medium, or 18 for well done). Add remaining marinade from time to time. Transfer meat to a hot platter. Discard bay leaf, skim the fat off and purée gravy in a blender, or force through a sieve. Taste for seasoning. If too thick, add a little water. Add the mushrooms and green peas; heat, and serve in a sauceboat.

Serve with a red Bordeaux or Burgundy, especially a Beaujolais, or an Italian red wine like Chianti, or a Rhône wine like Châteauneuf-du-Pape, or any American red wine.

Serves 8-10

RIB ROAST IN WINE

5-pound rolled rib roast
1/4 cup flour
4 tablespoons butter
1 cup chopped onion
1/2 cup chopped carrot
1 clove garlic, minced

2 tablespoons warm
  cognac
2 cups dry red wine
2 teaspoons salt
8 crushed peppercorns
1 bay leaf
1/2 teaspoon marjoram

Rub the meat with the flour. Heat the butter in a Dutch oven or heavy casserole; brown the meat in it on all sides. Add the chopped onion, carrot, and garlic, and cook until browned. Add the cognac and set aflame. When flames die down, add the wine, salt, peppercorns, bay leaf, and marjoram. Cover, and bake in a 325° oven about 3 hours, or until meat is tender.

Transfer the meat to a hot platter. Taste the gravy for seasoning, strain, and serve in a gravy boat.

Serve with a red Burgundy or Bordeaux, or an American red wine.

Serves 8-10

COSTA DI MANZO AL VINO ROSSO
(marinated roast beef, Italian style)

3-rib roast
3 cups dry red wine
3/4 cup sliced onion
1/2 cup sliced carrot
2 cloves garlic, minced

2 bay leaves
1/2 teaspoon freshly
  ground black pepper
2 1/2 teaspoons salt

Marinate the meat in a mixture of the wine, onion, carrot, garlic, bay leaves, and pepper for 24 hours in the refrigerator, basting and turning the meat several times.

Drain, reserving the marinade. Dry the meat with paper towels; rub with the salt. Place in a shallow roasting pan; roast in a 450° oven 20 minutes. Meanwhile, cook the marinade until reduced to half; pour over the meat. Roast a total of 15 minutes a pound, basting frequently. Skim the fat from the gravy, and serve gravy in a sauceboat.

Serve with a red Bordeaux or Burgundy, a Rhône wine like Châteauneuf-du-Pape, or a dry Italian red wine like Barolo, or a dry American red wine.

Serves 4-6

FILLET OF BEEF IN VERMOUTH

2 tablespoons butter	1 tablespoon flour
4 fillets of beef, cut 1 inch thick	1/4 cup dry vermouth
3/4 teaspoon salt	1/2 cup heavy cream

1/4 teaspoon freshly
    ground black pepper
	2 tablespoons chopped
	    parsley

Melt the butter in a skillet; brown the fillets in it over high heat, 2 minutes on each side, shaking the pan a few times. Sprinkle the meat with the salt and pepper, and stir the flour into the pan juices; add the vermouth and cream. Cook over medium heat 4 minutes longer, or to desired degree of rareness; turn the fillets once.

Arrange the fillets on a hot serving dish and pour the sauce over them. Sprinkle with the parsley.

Serve with a red Rhône wine like Châteauneuf-du-Pape, a dry Italian red wine like Valpolicella or Bardolino, or a dry American red wine.

Serves 4

FILET MIGNON AU PORTO
(filet of beef in port)

3 tablespoons butter	1/2 cup port

4 fillets of beef, cut
    1 inch thick
	1/2 cup sliced sautéed
	    mushrooms

1 teaspoon salt	3 tablespoons heavy cream
1/4 teaspoon freshly ground black pepper	

Melt the butter in a skillet; brown the fillets in it over high heat 3 minutes on each side, or to desired degree of rareness. Season with the salt and pepper and transfer to a heated serving dish; keep hot.

Stir the port, mushrooms, and cream into the pan juices; cook over low heat 3 minutes. Pour over the fillets.

Serve with a dry red Burgundy or Bordeau, or a dry red American wine.

Serves 4

BOEUF AU MADÈRE
(beef in Madeira)

3 pounds eye round of
    beef
2 teaspoons salt
1/4 teaspoon freshly
    ground black pepper
2 cloves garlic, minced
3 slices bacon, half cooked
2 cups thinly sliced onions
12 small carrots, scraped

1 pound mushrooms,
    sliced
2 teaspoons finely
    chopped bay leaf
1/4 cup minced parsley
1/4 pound cooked ham,
    chopped
1 1/2 cups Madeira wine
1/4 cup cognac

Cut the beef in 1-inch slices; trim off all the fat. Rub
meat with a mixture of the salt, pepper, and garlic. Arrange the sliced bacon on the bottom of a heavy deep casserole. Spread 1/3 the sliced onion, carrots, mushrooms,
bay leaves, parsley, and chopped ham over the bacon.
Arrange 4 slices of beef over it, then repeat the layers twice
more. Add the Madeira. Heat the cognac in a ladle, set
aflame, and pour into the casserole. When flames die,
cover, bring to a boil, and cook over low heat 2 1/2 hours.
Shake casserole occasionally.

Serve with a red Bordeaux or Burgundy, a Rhône wine
like Hermitage, an Italian red wine like Barolo, or any red
American wine.

Serves 6-8

FILETTO SICILIANA
(sautéed fillet of beef in marsala)

3 tablespoons butter
1 tablespoon olive oil
3/4 cup sliced onion
4 fillets of beef, cut
    1 inch thick
1 1/4 teaspoons salt

1/2 teaspoon freshly
    ground black pepper
1/3 cup Marsala or sherry
1/4 cup water
1 tablespoon minced
    parsley

Heat 2 tablespoons butter and the oil in a skillet; sauté
the onion slices 10 minutes, then remove. In the fat remaining, cook the fillets over high heat 2 minutes on each
side. Stir in the remaining butter, the salt, pepper, wine,
water, parsley, and sautéed onion slices. Cook 4 minutes

longer, or to desired degree of rareness. Turn the meat once.

Serve with a dry red Bordeaux or Burgundy, or a dry American red wine.

Serves 4

ITALIAN BEEF IN WHITE WINE

4 pounds chuck or rump of beef	1/2 cup sliced carrot
2 1/2 teaspoons salt	1/4 cup wine vinegar
1/2 teaspoon freshly ground black pepper	1 1/2 cups dry white wine
1 clove garlic, minced	1 1/2 pounds tomatoes, peeled and chopped
2 tablespoons butter	2 bay leaves
1 cup thinly sliced onion	1/4 teaspoon sugar
	1/4 cup heavy cream

Rub the meat with the salt, pepper, and garlic. Melt the butter in a Dutch oven or heavy saucepan; add the meat, sliced onion, and carrot. Cook over medium heat until meat is browned on all sides. Add the vinegar, wine, tomatoes, bay leaves, and sugar. Cover, and cook over low heat 2 1/2 hours, or until meat is tender. Taste for seasoning.

Pour off the gravy, and discard the bay leaves. Purée the gravy in a blender, or force through a sieve. If too thin, cook over high heat a few minutes. Stir in the cream. Slice the beef, and pour gravy over it.

Serve with a dry Italian red wine like Chianti or Bardolino, a Beaujolais, a red Rhône wine like Côte-Rôtie, or a dry red American wine.

Serves 6-8

FILETTO AL PÂTÉ
(fillet of beef with pâté)

6 fillets of beef, cut 1 1/2 inches thick	2 tablespoons butter
1 1/2 teaspoons salt	1/4 cup Marsala or sweet sherry
1/2 teaspoon freshly ground black pepper	4-ounce can *pâté de foie gras*
2 tablespoons olive oil	1/4 cup warmed cognac

Season the fillets with the salt and pepper, and rub with the oil. Let stand at room temperature 1 hour.

Melt the butter in a skillet; cook the fillets over high heat 1 minute on each side, or until browned. Remove. Stir the wine and *pâté* into the pan juices, stirring until smooth. Return the fillets; cook 2 minutes. Pour the cognac over them and set aflame; shake the pan until flames die. Transfer steaks to a serving dish, and pour the sauce over them.

Serve with a red Bordeaux or Burgundy, a red Rhône wine like Hermitage, a dry Italian red wine like Valpolicella, or a dry red American wine.

Serves 6

FILET DE BOEUF FARCI
(stuffed fillet of beef)

3-pound fillet of beef
2 1/2 teaspoons salt
3/4 teaspoon freshly ground black pepper
4 truffles, quartered
1 cup Madeira or sweet sherry
6 tablespoons butter
3/4 cup chopped onion
3/4 cup chopped carrot
1/2 cup chopped celery
1/4 cup chopped cooked ham

3 tablespoons minced parsley
1/8 teaspoon thyme
1/8 teaspoon finely chopped bay leaf
4-ounce can *pâté de foie gras*
1 tablespoon cognac
1 tablespoon vegetable oil
2 cups beef broth
1 tablespoon cornstarch

The fillet should weigh 3 pounds after it is trimmed. Do not have any fat wrapped around it, but ask the butcher for a piece of beef suet or pork fat the length of the beef and about 2 inches wide. Cut a deep slit lengthwise on the least attractive side, leaving both ends intact. Season the slit with a little of the salt and pepper.

Marinate the truffles in 1/3 cup of the Madeira for 30 minutes, with cup covered.

Melt 3 tablespoons of the butter in a small saucepan; add the chopped onion, carrot, celery, ham, parsley, thyme, bay leaf, 1/2 teaspoon of the salt, and 1/8 teaspoon pepper. Cover, and cook over low heat 10 minutes, but do not let brown. Add 1/3 cup of the Madeira; cook over high heat until wine is almost evaporated.

Mash the *pâté*, and beat in the cognac and 1 tablespoon of remaining wine. Spread in the slit of the fillet. Drain the truffles (reserve marinade) and arrange in a row on the *pâté* mixture. Close the slit and cover with the fat; tie securely with thread at close intervals.

In a casserole or heavy pan, heat the oil and 2 tablespoons of the butter. Brown the fillet in it lightly on all sides. Pour off the fat. Sprinkle with the remaining salt and pepper. Spread the cooked vegetables over the meat and add the broth. Bring to a boil, cover, and bake in a 350° oven 40 minutes (rare) or to desired degree of rareness. Baste a few times. Remove the meat, cut the thread, and discard the fat. Place slit side down on a hot serving platter.

Pour the pan juices into a saucepan. Skim off the fat. Add the truffle marinade. Cook over high heat 5 minutes. Mix the cornstarch with the remaining Madeira, stir into the sauce with the remaining butter until thickened, then cook 3 minutes longer. Taste for seasoning.

Cut the fillet into 3/4-inch slices, pour a little sauce over it, and serve the rest in a sauceboat.

Serve with a red Bordeaux or Burgundy, a red Rhône wine like Châteauneuf-du-Pape, or a red American wine.

Serves 8

FILET MIGNON AUX CHAMPIGNONS
(fillet of beef with mushrooms)

6 tablespoons butter	1 cup heavy cream
1 pound mushrooms, sliced	6 fillets of beef, 3/4 inch thick
2 tablespoons flour	1/3 cup Madeira or sweet sherry
2 teaspoons salt	
1/2 teaspoon freshly ground black pepper	

Melt 3 tablespoons butter in a skillet; sauté the mushrooms 5 minutes. Stir in the flour, 1 teaspoon of the salt, and 1/4 teaspoon pepper. Add the cream, stirring steadily to the boiling point. Reduce heat. Cook over low heat 5 minutes.

Melt the remaining butter in a skillet, and cook the fillets over high heat 3 minutes on each side. Season with remaining salt and pepper, add the wine, and bring to a boil.

To serve, arrange mushroom mixture in the center of a serving dish with the fillets around it.

Serve with a Beaujolais, a dry red Bordeaux, a dry Italian red wine like Valpolicella, or a dry red American wine.

Serves 6

FILET DE BOEUF PÔELÉ
(pan-roasted fillet of beef)

1 tablespoon olive oil
4-5-pound fillet of beef
1 carrot, sliced
3/4 cup sliced onion
1 cup Brown Sauce
  (see recipe)
1/2 cup Madeira or
  sweet sherry

Heat the oil in a Dutch oven or heavy roasting pan; cook the meat in it over high heat until browned on all sides. Add the carrot and onion, and brown lightly. Add the Brown Sauce and wine. Cover. Roast in a 375° oven, allowing 12 minutes a pound for rare meat, 15 for medium, and 18 for well done. Baste occasionally. Put meat on a hot serving platter. Skim fat from pan juices, taste for seasoning, and serve in a sauceboat.

Serve with a red Bordeaux or Burgundy, a red Rhône wine like Châteauneuf-du-Pape, a dry Italian red wine like Grignolino, or any dry red American wine.

Serves 8-10

LOMO DE TORO
(marinated fillets of beef)

6 fillets of beef, cut
  1 inch thick
1/3 cup olive oil
1 cup dry red wine
2 tablespoons wine
  vinegar
2 cloves garlic, minced
1 teaspoon salt
1/2 teaspoon freshly
  ground black pepper
2 tablespoons flour
3 tablespoons butter

Pound the beef lightly with a mallet or knife. Mix together the oil, wine vinegar, garlic, salt, and pepper; marinate the meat in it 4–6 hours, turning and basting frequently Drain the meat, and dry on paper towels.

Mix the flour with a little of the marinade. Combine with all the marinade in a saucepan. Bring to a boil over low heat, stirring steadily, then cook 5 minutes longer.

Melt the butter in a skillet; cook the fillets in it over high heat 2 minutes on each side, or to desired degree of rareness. Serve the sauce in a sauceboat.

Serve with a dry red Bordeaux wine, a red Burgundy, including a Beaujolais, a dry Italian red wine like Chianti, or any dry red American wine.

Serves 6

MANZO BRASATO
(braised beef in red wine)

4 pounds eye round,
    or rump of beef
4 tablespoons olive oil
1 tablespoon butter
2 cups dry red wine
1 1/2 cups chopped onion
1/2 cup grated carrot
1/2 cup diced celery
2 cloves garlic, minced
2 teaspoons salt
1/2 teaspoon freshly
    ground black pepper
1/2 teaspoon rosemary
1 bay leaf
Dash ground cloves
1 1/2 cups diced tomatoes

Have the beef larded. Put all the ingredients in a Dutch oven or heavy saucepan. Cover tightly, bring to a boil, and cook over low heat 2 1/2 hours or until tender. Discard bay leaf. Transfer the meat to a baking pan; purée the vegetables and gravy in a blender, or force through a sieve. Pour over the meat. Bake in 450° oven 15 minutes.

Serve with a red Burgundy or Bordeaux, a red Rhône wine like Côte-Rôtie, a red Italian wine like Chianti, or an American red wine.

Serves 6-8

BEEF BOURGUIGNONNE
(beef in red wine)

4 pounds rump or chuck
    of beef
1/2 cup flour
2 1/2 teaspoons salt
1/2 teaspoon freshly
    ground black pepper
3 tablespoons olive oil
6 tablespoons butter
1/4 cup warmed cognac
2 slices salt pork, diced
2 cups diced onions
1 cup grated carrot
2 cloves garlic, minced
3 1/2 cups dry red wine
2 tablespoons minced
    parsley
2 tablespoons finely
    chopped bay leaves
1/2 teaspoon marjoram
16 small white onions
1 teaspoon sugar
16 mushroom caps

Cut the meat into 2-inch cubes; roll in a mixture of the flour, salt, and pepper. Heat the oil and 2 tablespoons butter in a skillet; brown the meat very well on all sides. Transfer to a casserole; pour the warmed cognac over it and set aflame.

Brown the salt pork in a skillet. Remove and add to the casserole. Pour off all but 2 tablespoons fat. In the remaining fat, sauté the diced onion slices, carrot, and garlic 5 minutes. Add to the meat, with the wine, parsley, bay leaves, and marjoram. Bring to a boil over direct heat, then cover and bake in a 350° oven 1 hour.

Melt the remaining butter in a skillet; add the onions and sugar. Brown lightly and remove. Sauté the mushrooms in the remaining butter 5 minutes. Add to the meat; re-cover, and bake 30 minutes longer, or until meat is tender. Taste for seasoning.

Serve with a red Burgundy, including a Beaujolais, a red Rhône wine like Châteauneuf-du-Pape, or an American red wine.

Serves 8-10

STUFATO DI MANZO
(beef with white wine)

3 pounds eye round, cross rib, or rump	1 1/2 cups dry white wine
4 tablespoons butter	1 cup peeled, diced tomatoes
3 cups thinly sliced onions	3/4 cup sliced carrots
2 teaspoons salt	1/2 cup sliced celery
1/2 teaspoon freshly ground black pepper	1/2 teaspoon basil

Rinse the meat and pat dry. Melt the butter in a Dutch oven or heavy skillet; sauté the sliced onions until soft and yellow. Add the meat, and brown it on all sides. Season with the salt and pepper. Add the wine; cook over high heat 5 minutes. Add the tomatoes, carrots, celery, and basil. Bring to a boil, cover, and cook over low heat 2 hours, or until the meat is tender. Slice the meat and serve with the gravy.

Serve with a red Bordeaux or Burgundy, a Rhône wine like Côte-Rôtie, a dry Italian red wine like Barolo, or a dry American red wine.

Serves 6-8

ESTOUFFAT CATALAN
(braised stew, Catalan style)

5-pound eye round of beef
2 cloves garlic, slivered
4 strips of salt pork
1/4 cup vinegar
1/2 cup flour
1 1/2 cups thinly sliced onion
2 carrots, cut in matchlike strips
2 small white turnips, peeled and quartered
3 tomatoes, peeled and diced
3 sprigs parsley ⎱ tied
1 bay leaf ⎰ together
1/2 teaspoon thyme
2 cloves
2 teaspoons salt
1/2 teaspoon freshly ground black pepper
1 quart dry red wine
2 cups cooked or canned white beans

Cut a few slits in the beef and insert the garlic slivers, then wrap with the salt pork. Brush the meat with the vinegar and roll it in the flour. In a heavy deep casserole or Dutch oven, spread the onion slices, carrots, turnips, tomatoes, parsley and bay leaf, thyme, cloves, salt, and pepper. But the meat on top. Add the wine, bring to a boil over direct heat, cover pan tightly, and bake in a 275° oven 4 hours. When beef is almost cooked, add the beans and bake 10 minutes longer. Discard bay leaf and parsley.

Serve with a red Bordeaux or Burgundy, especially a Beaujolais, or a Rhône wine like Châteauneuf-du-Pape, an Italian red wine like Chianti, or an American red wine.

Serves 8-10

BOEUF EN MIROTON
(peasant beef stew)

2 tablespoons butter
2 tablespoons flour
1 cup beef broth
1 cup dry red wine
1 teaspoon salt
1/2 teaspoon freshly ground black pepper
12 small white onions
6 potatoes, peeled and quartered
2 sprigs parsley
1/4 teaspoon thyme
1 bay leaf
4 cups cooked beef, cut in 1/4-inch cubes

Melt the butter in a saucepan; blend in the flour until browned. Gradually mix in the broth and wine, stirring steadily to the boiling point. Add the salt and pepper, onions, potatoes, parsley, thyme, and bay leaf. Cook over

low heat 45 minutes. Add the beef. Cook 15 minutes.
longer. Discard parsley and bay leaf and serve.

Serve with a red Bordeaux or Burgundy, a red Rhône
wine like Côte-Rôtie, a red Italian wine like Grignolino,
or an American red wine.

Serves 6

LA CARBONNADE
(beef stew, Languedoc style)

2 tablespoons butter
3 pounds rump or sirloin
steak, cut into
1/2-inch cubes
1 cup sliced onion
2 tomatoes, peeled and
sliced thin
2 teaspoons salt
1/4 teaspoon freshly
ground pepper

2 cups cooked drained
rice
1 cup cooked or canned
corn kernels
1/2 cup finely sliced
green pepper
1/4 teaspoon saffron
1 teaspoon brown sugar
1 cup dry white wine
1/8 teaspoon cinnamon

Melt the butter in a casserole or Dutch oven; brown the
meat in it. Add the sliced onion and the tomatoes, salt and
pepper; cover, and cook over high heat 10 minutes, shaking pan frequently to prevent meat from sticking. Mix in
the rice and corn, green pepper, saffron, sugar, wine, and
cinnamon. Cover, and cook over low heat 15 minutes.
Taste for seasoning.

Serve with a red Bordeaux or a red Burgundy, including
a Beaujolais, a red Rhône wine like Châteauneuf-du-Pape,
an Italian red wine like Barolo, or an American red wine.

Serves 6

BOEUF À LA CATALANE
(beef stew with rice)

3 pounds rump or chuck
of beef
1/4 pound bacon
3 tablespoons olive oil
2 teaspoons salt
1/2 teaspoon freshly
ground black pepper
1 1/2 cups sliced onion
1 cup raw rice

1 cup dry white wine
2 cups beef broth
2 teaspoons finely
chopped bay leaves
1/2 teaspoon thyme
2 cloves garlic, minced
1/8 teaspoon saffron
1 1/2 cups peeled,
chopped tomatoes

Cut the beef in 2-inch squares, 1 inch thick. Cook the bacon slices in boiling water 10 minutes, drain, dry, and cut in 1-inch pieces. Brown the bacon in a skillet; drain, and transfer to a casserole. Pour off the fat. Heat the oil in the skillet; brown the meat in it. Transfer to the casserole. Sprinkle with the salt and pepper. In the fat remaining in the skillet, sauté the onion slices 5 minutes. Transfer to the casserole. To the fat remaining, add the rice. Cook over medium heat, stirring constantly, until rice is translucent. Remove rice and reserve.

Add the wine to the skillet; bring to a boil, scraping the bottom of any browned particles. Add to the casserole with the broth, bay leaves, thyme, garlic, and saffron. Bring to a boil, cover, and bake in a 325° oven 1 hour. Mix in the tomatoes; re-cover, and bake 1 1/2 hours longer.

Place over direct heat; lightly stir in the rice, and a little boiling water if necessary. At this point there should be about 2 1/2 cups liquid.) Re-cover, and cook over low heat 20 minutes, or until rice is tender. Taste for seasoning.

Serve with a red Bordeaux, a red Burgundy, including a Beaujolais, a Rhône wine like Côte-Rôtie, or a red American wine.

Serves 6-8

L'ESTOUFFAT DE BOEUF
(beef stew, Gascony style)

4-pound eye round of beef	(bouquet garni)
2 cloves garlic, slivered	1 onion, quartered
2 1/2 teaspoons salt	2 carrots, cut in long strips
1/2 teaspoon freshly ground black pepper	1 slice bacon, diced
1 slice salt pork	2 shallots
1/8 teaspoon cinnamon	1/4 cup cognac
1/8 teaspoon nutmeg	1/2 cup beef broth
3 cloves	2 cups dry red wine
Sprig parsley ⎫ Piece of celery ⎬ tied together Bay leaf ⎭	

Cut slits in the meat and insert the garlic slivers; rub the meat with the salt and pepper. Put the salt pork in a

large casserole or Dutch oven and place the beef over it.
Add the cinnamon, nutmeg, cloves, bouquet garni, onion,
carrots, diced bacon, shallots, cognac, broth, and wine. The
liquid should almost cover the meat. Cover casserole with
a piece of aluminum foil and tie securely. Cover with lid,
and roast in a 350° oven 1 hour. Reduce heat to 250° and
roast 5 hours longer. Skim fat from gravy before serving.
If you like, prepare the meat the day before it is to be
served and reheat—the flavor will be even better.

Serve with a dry red Bordeaux or Burgundy, a dry
Italian red wine like Bardolino, a red Rhône wine like
Châteauneuf-du-Pape, or a dry red American wine.

BOEUF EN DAUBE

4 pounds chuck or rump of beef	1/4 pound salt pork, diced
3 tablespoons flour	1/2 cup chopped onion
1 teaspoon salt	1/2 cup grated carrot
1/2 teaspoon freshly ground black pepper	2 cups dry red wine
	1 cup beef broth
1/8 teaspoon nutmeg	1/2 teaspoon thyme
	1 bay leaf

Cut the beef in 1 1/2-inch cubes. Toss in a mixture of the
flour, salt, pepper, and nutmeg.

Brown the salt pork in a Dutch oven or casserole; drain
off all but 3 tablespoons fat. Add the onion, carrot, and
beef; cook over medium heat until well browned. Add the
wine, broth, thyme, and bay leaf. Cover, and cook over
low heat 1 1/2 hours, or until the meat is tender. Skim off
the fat; taste for seasoning.

Serve with a heavy red Bordeaux, Beaujolais or other
red Burgundy, a red Rhône like Châteauneuf-du-Pape, a
dry red Italian wine like Barolo, or a dry red American
wine.

Serves 8-10

RAGOÛT DE BOEUF BORDELAISE
(marinated beef stew)

1 clove garlic, minced	2 cloves
2 teaspoons salt	1 bay leaf
1/2 teaspoon freshly ground black pepper	1/4 teaspoon thyme
	1 cup dry red wine

3 pounds chuck or rump
 of beef, cut in 2-inch
 cubes
1/2 cup flour
1/4 cup olive oil
2 cups beef broth

3 sprigs parsley
12 small white onions
1 1/2 cups sliced carrots
12 mushroom caps
1 cup cooked green beans

In a glass or pottery bowl, combine the garlic, salt, pepper, cloves, bay leaf, thyme, and wine. Add the meat and marinate 4 hours, or overnight if possible. Drain the meat, reserving the marinade. Toss the meat with the flour.

Heat the oil in a deep casserole or Dutch oven; add meat, and cook over low heat until very dark brown. Mix in the reserved marinade, broth, and parsley; bring to a boil, and cook over high heat 15 minutes. Reduce heat, cover, and cook over low heat 30 minutes. Add the onions, carrots, and mushrooms. Re-cover, and cook over low heat 1 1/2 hours, or until meat is tender. Mix in beans, taste for seasoning, and cook 2 minutes.

Serve with a red Bordeaux, a dry red Burgundy wine, including a Beaujolais, a red Italian wine like Valpolicella, or a dry red American wine.

Serves 6-8

CARBONADA CRIOLLA
(meat and fruit stew, South American style)

4 tablespoons olive oil
2 tablespoons butter
2 pounds beef, cut in
 1-inch cubes
1 pound veal, cut in
 1-inch cubes
1 1/2 cups diced onion
1 1/2 cups dry white wine
1 tablespoon tomato
 paste
1 bay leaf
2 teaspoons salt

1/2 teaspoon freshly
 ground black pepper
1/2 teaspoon thyme
1 cup beef broth
2 cups cubed sweet
 potatoes
2 pears, cubed
2 peaches or apples,
 peeled and sliced
3 tablespoons seedless
 raisins
1/2 cup diced bananas

Heat the oil and butter in a heavy casserole; brown the beef and veal in it. Remove meat. Brown the onion in the fat remaining in the pan. Return the meat, and stir in the wine, tomato paste, bay leaf, salt, pepper, thyme, and broth. Bring to a boil, cover, and cook over low heat 1 hour. Add the sweet potatoes; re-cover, and cook 30 minutes. Carefully mix in the pears, peaches, or apples, and raisins. Cook 10 minutes. Taste for seasoning, sprinkle with the bananas, and serve with rice.

Serve with a red Bordeaux or Burgundy, or an American or Italian red wine.

Serves 8-10

BOEUF À LA MODE

5 pounds rump, sirloin tip, or eye round	4 cups dry red wine
	1/4 cup cognac
2 1/2 teaspoons salt	1/4 cup olive oil
1/4 teaspoon freshly ground black pepper	2 tablespoons vegetable oil
1 cup thinly sliced onion	2 cups beef broth
1 cup sliced carrot	1 veal knuckle, cracked
2 cloves garlic, sliced	1 teaspoon Worcestershire sauce
2 teaspoons thyme	
1/4 cup minced parsley	1 tablespoon cornstarch
2 bay leaves	2 tablespoons sweet sherry

Have the beef larded; rub with the salt and pepper. In a large glass or pottery bowl, spread half the onion, carrot, garlic, thyme, parsley, and bay leaves. Put the meat in the bowl and cover with the remaining vegetables and herbs. Mix together the red wine, cognac, and olive oil; pour over the meat. Cover, and marinate in the refrigerator 24 hours, or 5 hours at room temperature. Turn and baste meat frequently. Drain the meat thoroughly, then dry with paper towels. Heat the marinade.

Heat the vegetable oil in a Dutch oven or heavy casserole; brown the meat on all sides. Pour off the fat. Add the heated marinade. Cook over high heat until marinade is reduced to half. Add the broth and veal knuckle. Bring to a boil, skim the top, cover, and bake in a 325° oven 3 1/2 hours, turning the meat several times. Transfer the meat to a heated serving dish and keep warm; discard veal knuckle and bay leaves. Mix the Worcestershire sauce, cornstarch, and sherry until smooth; stir into the gravy until thickened. Serve in a sauceboat. Sautéed small white onions and braised carrot quarters may be arranged around the meat, if desired.

Serve with a red Burgundy, especially Beaujolais, a red Rhône wine like Châteauneuf-du-Pape, an Italian red wine like Bardolino, or an American red wine.

Serves 10-12

STUFATINO ALLA ROMANA
(beef stew, Roman style)

3 pounds eye round of beef	2 slices salt pork, diced
3 tablespoons flour	2 tablespoons butter
2 teaspoons salt	1 cup thinly sliced onion
1/2 teaspoon freshly ground black pepper	2 cloves garlic, minced
	1 cup dry red wine
1/2 teaspoon rosemary	1 tablespoon tomato paste
	1/2 cup boiling water

Cut the meat in 1-inch slices. Sprinkle with the flour, salt, pepper, and rosemary. Lightly brown the salt pork in a heavy casserole. Pour off all but 2 tablespoons of the fat. Add the butter, onion slices, and garlic; sauté 5 minutes. Add the meat; cook over medium heat until browned on both sides. Stir in the wine; cook over high heat 5 minutes. Blend in the tomato paste, mixed with the water. Cover, and cook over low heat 1 1/2 hours. Taste for seasoning.

Serve with any Italian red wine, especially Chianti or Bardolino, a red Bordeaux or Burgundy, a red Rhône wine like Châteauneuf-du-Pape, or a red American wine.

Serves 6-8

LE HACHUA
(braised beef)

1/4 cup olive oil	1 bay leaf
3 pounds rump or chuck of beef, cut in 1-inch cubes	1/2 teaspoon thyme
	2 teaspoons salt
2 tablespoons flour	1/2 teaspoon freshly ground pepper
2 cups chopped onion	
2 cloves garlic, minced	1 cup hot water
1 1/2 cups finely diced ham	1 1/2 cups dry white wine
	3 green peppers, cut julienne
3 sprigs parsley	

Heat the oil in a casserole or Dutch oven; brown the beef in it on all sides. Blend in the flour; add onion, garlic, ham, parsley, bay leaf, thyme, salt, and pepper. Cook 5 minutes, stirring frequently. Gradually stir in the water and wine. Cover tightly, and bake in a 275° oven 2 hours. Add the green peppers; re-cover and bake 30 minutes longer, or until the meat is tender.

Serve with a red Bordeaux or Burgundy, especially a Beaujolais, a Rhône red wine like Hermitage, a dry Italian red wine like Chianti, or a dry red American wine.

Serves 6-8

GRYTSTEK
(Swedish pot roast)

4 pounds eye round or rump of beef	1/4 cup cognac
2 1/2 teaspoons salt	1 cup boiling water
3/4 teaspoon freshly ground black pepper	1 cup dry white wine
4 tablespoons butter	1/4 teaspoon allspice
1 1/2 cups chopped onion	2 bay leaves
2 carrots, sliced	2 teaspoons anchovy paste
1/4 cup molasses	1 tablespoon cider vinegar
	2 tablespoons flour
	1 1/2 cups light cream

Rub the meat with salt and pepper. Melt the butter in a Dutch oven or heavy saucepan; brown the meat well on all sides. Add the onion and carrot, and cook 10 minutes. Stir in the molasses, cognac, water, wine, allspice, bay leaves, anchovy paste, and vinegar. Cover, and cook over low heat 2 1/2 hours, or until tender. Transfer the meat to a heated platter. Mix the flour and cream until smooth; blend into the gravy, stirring steadily to the boiling point. Cook 5 minutes. Discard bay leaves, taste for seasoning, and serve gravy separately.

Serve with a red Burgundy, Bordeaux, a Rhône wine like Côte-Rôtie, an Italian or American red wine.

Serves 8-10

MANZO IN SALSA DI PREZZEMOLA
(beef with parsley sauce)

4 slices eye round of beef, cut 2 inches thick	4 anchovy fillets, chopped
2 tablespoons olive oil	1 clove garlic, minced
	1/4 cup chopped parsley

| 3/4 cup dry white wine | 1/4 teaspoon freshly |
| 1/2 teaspoon salt | ground black pepper |

Pound the beef with a mallet or cleaver to tenderize. Heat the oil in a skillet; brown the beef on both sides. Mix in the anchovies, garlic, and parsley; cook over low heat 5 minutes. Add the wine, salt, and pepper. Cover, and cook over low heat 30 minutes or until meat is tender.

Serve with any dry red Bordeaux or Burgundy, or any red American wine.

Serves 4

TOURNEDOS LYONNAISE
(beef tenderloin, Lyons style)

4 fillets of beef, cut 1 inch thick	4 slices sautéed French bread
1 1/2 teaspoons salt	2 tablespoons chopped shallots or onion
1/2 teaspoon freshly ground black pepper	1/2 cup dry white wine
4 tablespoons butter	1 teaspoon anchovy paste

Rub the fillets with salt and pepper. Melt 3 tablespoons of the butter in a skillet; cook the fillets in it over high heat 2 minutes on each side, or to desired degree of rareness. Place a fillet on a sautéed slice of bread. Keep hot. Add the shallots to butter remaining in the pan; sauté 1 minute. Stir in the wine, anchovy paste, and the remaining tablespoon butter. Cook 2 minutes, stirring frequently. Pour sauce over the fillets, and serve with sautéed potatoes.

Serve with a red Burgundy or Bordeaux, a dry red Italian wine like Bardolino, a red Rhône wine like Hermitage, or an American red wine.

Serves 4

CADERA DE TORO
(braised beef)

4 pounds eye round of beef	2 cups dry white wine
2 1/2 teaspoons salt	1 cup water
3/4 teaspoon freshly ground black pepper	2 teaspoons wine vinegar
2 cloves garlic, minced	2 cloves
1/4 cup olive oil	1 bay leaf
1 cup chopped onion	1 tablespoon unsweetened cocoa

Rub the meat with a mixture of the salt, pepper, and garlic. Heat the oil in a Dutch oven or heavy saucepan; brown the meat in it lightly. Add the chopped onions; cook 5 minutes, stirring frequently. Pour off the fat; add the wine, water, vinegar, cloves, and bay leaf. Cover, and cook over low heat 2 1/2 hours, or until the meat is tender. Turn meat a few times, and add a little boiling water if necessary. Transfer the meat to a hot platter. Strain the gravy into a saucepan; stir the cocoa into it. Cook 1 minute. Slice the meat, and pour the gravy over it.

Serve with a red Bordeaux or Burgundy, a dry Italian red wine like Valpolicella, a red Rhône wine like Hermitage, or an American red wine.

Serves 6-8

SWISS STEAK IN WINE SAUCE

1/4 cup flour	1 cup chopped onion
1 1/2 teaspoons salt	1 clove garlic, minced
1/4 teaspoon freshly ground black pepper	1 cup dry red wine
	1/2 teaspoon marjoram
4 pounds round steak	1 bay leaf
4 tablespoons butter	

Mix together the flour, salt, and pepper. Dip the steak in the mixture, then pound the mixture in. Melt the butter in a Dutch oven or heavy saucepan. Brown the steak in it on both sides. Add the onion and garlic. Continue browning for 5 minutes. Add the wine, marjoram, and bay leaf. Cover and cook over low heat for 2 hours, basting and turning the meat frequently. Taste for seasoning. Discard the bay leaf.

Serve with a red Bordeaux or Burgundy, any dry Italian red wine like Bardolino, or an American red wine.

Serves 6

BEEF BIRDS

1 1/2 pounds fillet of beef	1/8 teaspoon nutmeg
	1/4 pound ham, chopped
1 1/4 teaspoons salt	1/4 cup chopped parsley
1/2 teaspoon freshly ground black pepper	1/4 cup grated Swiss cheese
1/2 teaspoon thyme	3 tablespoons butter

1 clove garlic, minced
1 1/2 cups peeled,
   chopped tomatoes

1/4 pound mushrooms,
   sliced
1 bay leaf
3/4 cup dry white wine

Slice the beef as thin as possible, then pound between two sheets of waxed paper. Season one side with the salt, pepper, thyme, and nutmeg. On the unseasoned side, spread a mixture of the ham, parsley, and cheese. Roll up, and fasten with toothpicks or tie with white thread.

Melt the butter in a casserole or deep skillet; brown the meat rolls on all sides. Mix in the garlic, tomatoes, mushrooms, bay leaf, and wine. Bring to a boil, and cook over low heat 20 minutes. Taste for seasoning. Discard bay leaf.

Serve with any red Bordeaux or Burgundy, or an American red wine.

Serves 6-8

BEEF STROGANOFF

2 1/2 pounds fillet of
   beef
4 tablespoons butter
2 tablespoons vegetable
   oil
1/2 pound mushrooms,
   sliced
3 tablespoons minced
   shallots or green
   onions

1/2 cup Madeira or sweet
   sherry
1/4 cup beef broth
1 3/4 teaspoons salt
1/2 teaspoon freshly
   ground black pepper
1 cup sour cream

Trim the fat off the fillet. Slice 1/2 inch thick, then cut into pieces 2 inches long and 2 inches wide.

Heat 2 tablespoons butter and 1 tablespoon oil in a skillet; sauté the mushrooms over medium heat 3 minutes. Add the shallots; sauté 2 minutes. Remove from the skillet. Add the remaining butter and oil to the skillet. Bring to a boil, then add the meat. Brown quickly over high heat. Remove the meat, and pour off the fat.

Mix the wine and broth into the skillet, scraping the bottom well; cook over high heat 2 minutes. Season the meat with the salt and pepper, then return to the skillet with the mushrooms. Cook over low heat 5 minutes, stirring frequently. Just before serving, blend in sour cream. Heat, but do not let boil.

Serve with a red Bordeaux or Burgundy, or an American red wine.

Serves 4-6

NOODLES WITH STROGANOFF SAUCE

4 tablespoons butter
1/4 cup chopped green onions
1 clove garlic, minced
1/2 pound mushrooms, sliced
1 pound ground beef
2 tablespoons lemon juice
1 cup dry red wine
1/4 cup beef broth

1 teaspoon salt
1/4 teaspoon freshly ground black pepper
1/2 pound medium noodles, half cooked and drained
1 cup sour cream
3 tablespoons chopped parsley

Melt the butter in a large skillet; sauté the green onions, garlic, and mushrooms 5 minutes. Add the beef; cook over medium heat, stirring almost constantly, until meat browns. Mix in the lemon juice, wine, broth, salt, and pepper. Bring to a boil, and cook over low heat 15 minutes. Add the half-cooked noodles; cover, and cook 5 minutes. Blend in the sour cream, taste for seasoning, and reheat, but do not let boil. Sprinkle with the parsley.

Serve with a *rosé* wine, or any light dry red wine.

Serves 4

BEEF AND PRUNES WITH SPAGHETTI

1/2 cup olive oil
1 cup chopped onion
2 cloves garlic, minced
1 pound beef, cut in 1/2-inch cubes
2 8-ounce cans tomato sauce
3/4 cup dry red wine

1/2 teaspoon salt
1/2 teaspoon nutmeg
12 prunes, pre-soaked and pitted
1 pound spaghetti, cooked and drained
1/2 cup grated Parmesan cheese

Heat the oil in a saucepan; sauté the onion, garlic, and beef until browned, stirring frequently. Add the tomato sauce, wine, salt, and nutmeg. Cook over low heat 40 minutes. Add the prunes. Cook 30 minutes. Taste for seasoning.

Heap the cooked spaghetti on a platter and pour the meat mixture over it. Serve with the cheese.

Serve with any dry red Bordeaux or Burgundy, or an American red wine.

Serves 4-6

BEEF AND MACARONI CASSEROLE

1/4 cup olive oil	1/2 teaspoon basil
1 1/2 cups chopped onion	1 cup sliced almonds
1 clove garlic, minced	3 eggs
1 1/2 pounds ground beef	1/2 cup grated Parmesan cheese
1 cup peeled chopped tomatoes	1 pound elbow marcaroni, cooked and drained
3/4 cup dry red wine	2 egg yolks
2 1/2 teaspoons salt	1/2 cup cream
1/4 teaspoon freshly ground black pepper	

Heat the olive oil in a skillet; sauté the onion and garlic 10 minutes. Add beef and sauté 10 minutes, stirring almost constantly. Mix in the tomatoes, wine, 1 1/2 teaspoons salt, the pepper, and basil. Cook over medium heat 15 minutes. Stir in the almonds.

Beat the eggs; stir in the cheese and spaghetti. Spread half the spaghetti mixture in a 2-quart buttered casserole. Spread the meat mixture over it. Cover with the remaining spaghetti mixture. Beat together the egg yolks, cream, and remaining salt, and pour over top. Bake in a 350° oven 25 minutes, or until custard is set and lightly browned.

Serve with a dry red Italian wine like Barolo, a red Bordeaux or Burgundy, or a red American wine.

Serves 6-8

STEAK DIANE

2 8-ounce club steaks, cut 1/4 inch thick	2 tablespoons warm cognac
1 teaspoon dry mustard	1/3 cup dry sherry
2 tablespoons A.1. Sauce	1 tablespoon chopped chives or green onions
4 tablespoons butter	

Trim the steaks, then rub with a mixture of the mustard and A.1. Sauce. Melt 2 tablespoons butter in a skillet or chafing dish. Add the steaks and cook over high heat 2 minutes on each side, or to desired degree of rareness. Set the cognac aflame in a ladle and pour over the steaks. Immediately add the sherry, chives, and remaining butter. Transfer the steaks to a hot serving dish, bring the sauce to a boil, and pour over the steaks.

Serve with a red Burgundy or Bordeaux, a red Rhône wine like Hermitage, an Italian red wine like Chianti, or an American red wine.

Serves 2

SLICED BEEF WITH CHICKEN LIVER SAUCE

2 pounds fillet of beef	1/4 teaspoon freshly
4 tablespoons butter	ground black pepper
1/2 pound chicken livers	1/3 cup dry sherry
1 bay leaf	1/4 cup beef broth
1 teaspoon salt	2 tablespoons cognac

Cut the meat in thin strips across the grain.

Melt 2 tablespoons butter in a skillet; sauté the livers and bay leaf over high heat 3 minutes. Sprinkle with the salt and pepper; sauté 2 minutes. Discard the bay leaf; purée the livers, sherry, and broth in an electric blender until smooth, or force through a food mill. Return purée to skillet, and keep it warm while preparing the meat.

Melt the remaining butter in a skillet; sauté the meat over high heat 2 minutes, shaking the pan frequently. Heat the cognac and pour over the meat; set aflame. Transfer the meat to a heated serving dish and pour the liver sauce over it.

Serve with an American red wine, a red Burgundy or Bordeaux, a red Rhône wine like Châteauneuf-du-Pape, or a dry Italian red wine like Grignolino or Barolo.

Serves 4-6

STEAK AND KIDNEY PIE

4 veal kidneys	3 tablespoons vegetable
2 pounds top round steak	oil
1/4 cup flour	1 cup thinly sliced onion

1/2 pound mushrooms, sliced	1/2 teaspoon thyme
2 teaspoons salt	1 tablespoon tomato paste
3/4 teaspoon freshly ground black pepper	1 cup dry red wine
	Pastry for 1-crust pie

Wash the kidneys, cut in half, and discard the core. Cover with boiling water, let stand 2 minutes, drain, and cube.

Cut the steak into 1 1/2-inch cubes. Toss the meat and kidneys with the flour. Heat the oil in a skillet; brown the meat and kidneys in it.

In a buttered 2-quart casserole, arrange layers of the sautéed meats, the sliced onion, and the mushrooms. Mix together the salt, pepper, thyme, tomato paste, and wine; pour into the casserole. Cover the casserole and bake in a 350° oven 2 1/2 hours.

Prepare the pastry and roll out a little larger than the casserole. Taste casserole contents for seasoning. Carefully place the pastry over the meat mixture and press the edges down with a fork. Make a few gashes in the top. Increase the heat to 400° and bake 25 minutes longer, or until the pastry is browned.

Serve with a red Bordeaux or Burgundy, an Italian red wine like Valpolicella, or an American red wine.

Serves 4-6

MEAT BALL CASSEROLE

4 tablespoons butter	1/2 teaspoon thyme
1 cup chopped onion	2 tablespoons vegetable oil
1 clove garlic, minced	
1/2 cup dry bread crumbs	1 pound mushrooms, sliced
2 pounds ground beef	
2 eggs, beaten	1 10 1/2-ounce can cream of mushroom soup
2 teaspoons salt	
1/2 teaspoon freshly ground black pepper	2 cups dry white wine

Melt 2 tablespoons butter in a skillet; sauté the onion 10 minutes. Mix in the garlic and bread crumbs; sauté 2 minutes. Remove from heat, and add the beef, eggs, salt, pepper, and thyme. Mix well. Shape into 2-inch balls.

Heat the oil and remaining butter in a skillet; brown

the meat balls in it. Transfer to a casserole or baking dish.
Sautée the mushrooms in the fat remaining in the skillet
for 3 minutes. Add to the casserole. Mix the soup and
wine; pour over the meat balls. Cover casserole; bake in
a 350° oven 45 minutes, removing the cover for the last
10 minutes. Taste for seasoning.

Serve with a red Bordeaux or a red Burgundy, including
a Beaujolais, an Italian red wine like Chianti, a red Rhône
wine like Hermitage, or an American red wine.

Serves 6-8

LUK AWALIANI
(meat-stuffed onions, Syrian style)

12 large onions	1/8 teaspoon nutmeg
3/4 pound ground beef	4 cups beef broth
3/4 pound ground lamb	2 1/2 cups strained
1/2 pound calf's or beef	canned
liver, ground	plum tomatoes
3/4 cup chopped mixed	1 cup chopped
nuts	mushrooms
1 1/2 teaspoons salt	1 cup sour cream
1/2 teaspoon freshly	1/2 cup sherry
ground black pepper	

Peel the onions and carefully remove as much of the
centers as possible. Reserve. Mix together the beef, lamb,
liver, nuts, salt, pepper, and nutmeg. Stuff the onions with
the mixture, piled high. Arrange in a baking pan. Pour the
broth and 2 cups tomatoes around them. Bake in a 350°
oven 1 hour. While they are baking, prepare the sauce.

Chop the onion centers, and combine in a saucepan
with the mushrooms, sour cream, sherry, and remaining
tomatoes. Cover, and cook over low heat 20 minutes. Add
to the onions. Bake 30 minutes longer, basting frequently.
Taste for seasoning.

Serve with any dry red wine.

Serves 6-12

CHIPPED BEEF WITH ARTICHOKE HEARTS

6 tablespoons butter	Salt, depending on the
6 tablespoons flour	saltiness of the
1 1/2 cups milk, scalded	chipped beef

2 cups sour cream
1/2 cup dry white wine
2 cups shredded chipped
    beef

1 package frozen artichoke
    hearts, cooked and
    drained
1 1/2 cups sliced ripe
    olives

Melt the butter in a saucepan; blend in the flour until smooth. Add the milk, stirring vigorously with a wire whisk. Cook until thick and smooth, then add the salt, sour cream, wine, beef, artichokes, and olives.

Heat, but do not boil. Serve hot with cooked rice.

Serve with any dry red Bordeaux or Burgundy, or an American red wine.

Serves 4

THREE-MEAT GOULASH

4 tablespoons butter
3 cups thinly sliced onions
1 pound boneless beef,
    cut in 1-inch cubes
1 pound boneless veal,
    cut in 1-inch cubes
1 pound boneless pork,
    cut in 1-inch cubes

2 teaspoons salt
1/2 teaspoon freshly
    ground black pepper
2 teaspoons paprika
2 tablespoons tomato
    paste
1 cup dry white wine
1 cup sour cream

Melt the butter in a casserole; sauté the sliced onions 10 minutes. Add all the meat, and cook over medium heat until browned. Stir in the salt, pepper, paprika, tomato paste, and 1/4 cup wine. Cover, and cook over low heat 30 minutes. Add the remaining wine, and cook 1 1/2 hours longer. Stir the sour cream into the pan juices. Heat, but do not let boil.

Serve with a red Bordeaux or Burgundy, an Italian red wine like Valpolicello, or an American red wine.

Serves 6-8

ROAST LEG OF LAMB

4-pound leg of lamb
3 cloves garlic, cut in
    slivers
3/4 teaspoon rosemary
2 1/2 teaspoons salt

3/4 teaspoon freshly
    ground black pepper
4 tablespoons butter
1 1/2 cups dry vermouth

Make a few slits in the lamb and insert the garlic and rosemary. Rub the leg with the salt and pepper. Place in a shallow roasting pan and dot with the butter. Roast in a 450° oven 25 minutes, or until browned. Pour off the fat. Add the vermouth. Reduce heat to 350°, and roast 1 hour longer, or until meat is tender; baste frequently.

Serve with any red Bordeaux or Burgundy.

Serves 4-6

MARINATED ROAST LAMB

4-5-pound leg of lamb	1 teaspoon rosemary
1 tablespoon salt	1/2 cup olive oil
3/4 teaspoon freshly	1/3 cup wine vinegar
ground black pepper	1 cup dry red wine

Trim the fat off the lamb. Prick the lamb in several places, then rub with the salt, pepper, and rosemary. Place in a large glass bowl, and pour over it a mixture of the oil, vinegar, and wine. Marinate in the refrigerator 8 hours, basting occasionally.

Drain, and place in a shallow roasting pan. Roast in a 350° oven, allowing 15 minutes a pound, or to desired degree of rareness. Add the marinade after 30 minutes roasting time, and baste frequently thereafter.

Serve with any red Bordeaux or Burgundy, or any dry American or Italian red wine.

Serves 6-8

ROAST CROWN OF LAMB

Crown of lamb	2 cups fresh bread crumbs
1/2 teaspoon thyme	1/2 cup melted butter
3 teaspoons salt	2 cloves garlic, minced
3/4 teaspoon freshly	1 potato cube or salt pork
ground black pepper	1 1/2 cups dry sherry
1/2 cup minced onion	Sautéed mushroom caps

Have the butcher shape a crown for you—it will require 16 ribs, so plan to serve it for at least 8 people. Have the bones scraped, and the meat from them ground. Mix the ground meat with the thyme, 3/4 teaspoon salt, 1/4 teaspoon pepper, the minced onion, bread crumbs, and 1/4 cup of the melted butter.

Rub the crown with a mixture of the garlic and remaining salt and pepper. Place in a roasting pan and fill the center with the stuffing. Cover the stuffing with a piece of aluminum foil. Place a potato cube or a piece of salt pork on each bone to keep ends from burning. Roast in a 450° oven 20 minutes. Pour off the fat, and add the remaining butter and sherry. Reduce heat to 350°, and roast 2 hours longer, or to desired degree of rareness. Baste frequently, and remove foil from stuffing for last 15 minutes of roasting time. Transfer to a heated platter, remove potato or pork and replace each piece with a mushroom cap. Skim the fat from the gravy, and serve gravy with the roast.

Serve with any red Bordeaux or Burgundy, or American red wine.

Serves 8-10

ROAST SADDLE OF LAMB

7-pound loin of lamb, in one piece
2 1/2 teaspoons salt
3/4 teaspoon freshly ground black pepper
2 cloves garlic, minced
1 cup dry red wine

Have the flank ends rolled and tied by the butcher. Rub the lamb with a mixture of the salt, pepper, and garlic. Place in a shallow roasting pan. Roast in a 400° oven 20 minutes. Pour off the fat. Add the wine; roast 1 1/2 hours longer, or to desired degree of rareness, basting frequently. Carve parallel to the bones in long strips—don't cut into chops.

Serve with a red Bordeaux or Burgundy, or any dry American or Italian red wine.

Serves 6-8

KZARTMA
(shanks of lamb, Near East Style)

6 lamb shanks
1 cup chopped onion
2 tablespoons butter
1 tablespoon salt
1 teaspoon freshly ground black pepper
1/8 teaspoon oregano
2 tablespoons paprika
3 cloves garlic, minced
1 8-ounce can tomato sauce
1/2 cup beef broth
1/2 cup dry sherry

Soak the shanks in cold water for 1/2 hour. Drain, dry, and remove excess fat. Arrange in a shallow casserole or deep skillet with ovenproof handle.

Sauté the chopped onion in the butter and add to the lamb with the salt, pepper, oregano, paprika, garlic, tomato sauce, broth, and sherry. Cover, and bake in a 350° oven 1 1/2 hours, basting occasionally. Remove cover and continue baking in a 250° oven until lamb browns and is tender—about 45 minutes. Baste frequently. Serve with cracked wheat or rice.

Serve with a dry American red wine.

Serves 6-8

SHISH KABOB

1/4 cup dry red wine	1 tablespoon salt
1/4 cup olive oil	2 pounds boneless lamb,
2 tablespoons grated	cut in 1 1/2-inch
onion	cubes
1 teaspoon crushed	Sliced onions
coriander seeds	Sliced tomatoes
1 teaspoon ground ginger	Sliced green peppers
1 teaspoon turmeric	Mushroom caps
1 clove garlic, minced	1/2 cup melted butter

Mix together the wine, oil, grated onion, crushed coriander seeds, ginger, turmeric, garlic, and salt. Marinate the meat in the mixture for 2 hours. Use 6 skewers and alternately thread the meat, sliced onions, tomatoes, green peppers, and mushroom caps on them, starting and ending with meat. Broil over charcoal or in the oven broiler, turning the skewers frequently and basting with the butter. Broil 10 minutes, or to desired degree of rareness.

Note: Beef or pork are equally good prepared in this way.

Serve with any dry red wine.

Serves 6

ARMENIAN SHISH KABOB

1 1/2 pounds boneless leg	1 1/2 cups dry red wine
of lamb	1 1/3 cups sherry

1/4 teaspoon thyme
1/2 teaspoon marjoram
1/2 teaspoon Tabasco
1/2 teaspoon salt
2 onions, thinly sliced
18 small white onions

18 mushroom caps
18 squares green pepper
18 cubes eggplant
1/2 cup canned
   mushroom sauce

Cut the lamb in 1-inch cubes. In a glass or pottery bowl, combine the red wine, 1 cup sherry, thyme, marjoram, Tabasco, salt, and sliced onions. Add the meat. Marinate in the refrigerator 24 hours. Drain.

On 6 skewers, alternately thread the meat, white onions, mushrooms, green pepper, and eggplant. Mix the remaining sherry with the mushroom sauce, and brush the skewered ingredients.

Broil 15 minutes, turning the skewers frequently. Serve with rice.

Serve with any dry red wine.

Serves 6

LAMB IN SOUR–CREAM SAUCE

3 pounds boneless lamb,
   cut in 1-inch cubes
1/4 cup flour
2 teaspoons salt
1/2 teaspoon freshly
   ground black pepper
1/8 teaspoon rosemary

3 tablespoons butter
1 cup chopped onion
3 tablespoons dry sherry
1 cup dry white wine
1/2 cup beef broth
1 cup sour cream

Roll the lamb in a mixture of the flour, salt, pepper, and rosemary. Melt the butter in a Dutch oven or heavy skillet; brown the lamb in it. Pour off the fat. Mix in the chopped onions; cook over low heat 3 minutes. Add the sherry; cook until evaporated. Add the white wine and broth; cover, and cook over low heat 1 1/2 hours, or until the lamb is tender. Mix in the sour cream; taste for seasoning. Heat, but do not let boil.

Serve with a dry Italian red wine, or if you wish, with a *rosé*.

Serves 6-8

ABBACCHIO AL VERMOUTH
(lamb with artichokes in vermouth)

2 tablespoons butter
3 pounds shoulder of
lamb, cut in 1-inch
cubes
2 1/2 teaspoons salt
1/4 teaspoon freshly
ground black pepper
1/4 cup dry vermouth

1 package frozen artichoke
hearts, cooked and
drained
4 eggs
1/2 cup grated Parmesan
cheese
2 tablespoons minced
parsley

Melt the butter in a casserole or deep skillet with oven-proof handle. Brown the lamb in it. Season with 2 tea-spoons salt and the pepper. Add the wine; cook over high heat 5 minutes. Cover, and bake in a 350° oven 35 min-utes; add the artichokes, and a little boiling water if neces-sary. Re-cover, and bake 10 minutes.

Beat together the eggs, cheese, parsley, and remaining salt. Pour over the lamb and artichokes. Bake, uncovered, 10 minutes longer.

Serve with a red Bordeaux or Burgundy, or a *rosé*, or an American red wine.

Serves 6

AGNEAU À LA RHEIMS
(roast lamb in champagne sauce)

6-pound leg of lamb
1 tablespoon salt
1 teaspoon freshly
ground black pepper
1/4 cup flour

4 tablespoons butter
1/2 cup beef broth
1 1/2 cups champagne
1/2 cup grated onion
1 clove garlic, minced

Remove the fell (skin) of the lamb, and trim the fat. Rub the leg with a mixture of the salt, pepper, and flour. Place in a roasting pan, and dot with the butter. Roast in a 450° oven for 20 minutes. Combine the broth, champagne, grated onion, and garlic in a saucepan. Bring to a boil, and pour over the lamb. Reduce the heat to 350°, and con-tinue roasting for 2 1/2 hours, or until the lamb is tender, basting frequently. Skim the fat from the gravy, and serve gravy in a sauceboat.

Serve with champagne or a *rosé* wine.

Serves 6-8

AGNEAU AU VIN ROUGE
(lamb stew in red wine)

3 pounds boneless lamb, cut in 1 1/2-inch cubes	3 tablespoons butter
	3 tablespoons warmed cognac
1/4 cup flour	3 cups dry red wine
2 teaspoons salt	2 cups diced onions
1/4 teaspoon freshly ground black pepper	1 cup diced carrots
1/2 teaspoon thyme	1 bay leaf

Roll the lamb in a mixture of the flour, salt, pepper, and thyme. Melt the butter in a casserole; brown the meat in it. Pour the warmed cognac over the meat and set it aflame. When flames die, add the wine, diced onion, carrots, and bay leaf. Cover, and bake in a 350° oven 2 hours. Skim off the fat and discard the bay leaf. If gravy is too thin, add 1 tablespoon flour, kneaded with 1 tablespoon butter. Cook over direct heat until thickened.

Serve with any red Bordeaux or Burgundy, or an American red wine.

Serves 6-8

DAUBE À LA MODE D'AVIGNON
(lamb in red wine)

3 pounds boneless lamb	3 slices salt pork, diced
3 cups dry red wine	2 teaspoons salt
2 cloves garlic, minced	1/2 teaspoon freshly ground black pepper
1 1/2 cups diced onions	
3 teaspoons finely chopped bay leaves	1 cup peeled, diced tomatoes
3 peppercorns	3 tablespoons minced parsley
1/2 teaspoon thyme	

Cut the lamb in 1 1/2-inch cubes. Combine the wine, garlic, diced onions, bay leaves, peppercorns, and thyme in a glass or pottery bowl. Marinate the lamb in the mixture 8 hours, basting occasionally.

Brown the salt pork in a casserole or Dutch oven; pour off the fat. Drain the lamb, reserving the marinade, and season with the salt and pepper. Add to salt pork, and cook over medium heat 10 minutes. Mix in 2 cups of the reserved marinade, the tomatoes, and parsley; cover tightly, and bake in a 300° oven 3 hours, adding a little of the remaining marinade from time to time if necessary. Skim the fat off the gravy. Taste for seasoning.

Serve with a dry red American or Italian wine, or a red Bordeaux or Burgundy.

Serves 6-8

COSTOLETTE D'AGNELLO
(lamb chops in white wine)

4 shoulder lamb chops,
    cut 1 inch thick
1 1/2 teaspoons salt
1/2 teaspoon freshly
    ground black pepper
2 tablespoons flour
2 tablespoons butter
1 cup dry white wine

1/2 teaspoon rosemary
1 clove garlic, minced
1 teaspoon grated lemon
    rind
1 bay leaf
2 tablespoons minced
    parsley

Trim the fat off the lamb; rub the chops with a mixture of the salt, pepper, and flour. Melt the butter in a heavy skillet; brown the chops in it. Pour off the fat. Add the wine, rosemary, garlic, lemon rind, and bay leaf. Bring to a boil, cover, and cook over low heat 45 minutes, or until tender. Sprinkle with the parsley before serving.

Serve with a red Bordeaux or Burgundy, a white Rhône wine, a *rosé*, or an American red wine.

Serves 4

RESTES DE GIGOT À LA BRISSAC
(leftover lamb in white wine sauce)

2 tablespoons butter
8 slices roast lamb
    (leftovers)
2 tablespoons chopped
    onion
1 teaspoon chopped
    parsley

2 tablespoons flour
3/4 cup dry white wine
2 tablespoons olive oil
1 teaspoon salt
1/4 teaspoon freshly
    ground black pepper

Melt the butter in a skillet; brown the lamb slices in it on both sides. Add the chopped onion and parsley; sauté 5 minutes. Stir in the flour until browned. Add the wine, stirring steadily to the boiling point. Cover, and cook over medium heat 30 minutes. Add the olive oil, salt, and pepper, and cook 10 minutes longer. Taste for seasoning. Serve with boiled potatoes or boiled rice.

Serve with a red Bordeaux or Burgundy, a white Rhône wine, a *rosé*, or an American red wine.

Serves 4

CASSOULET

4 cups dried white beans	1 pound lamb, cubed
2 onions	1 1/2 cups chopped
2 cloves	onion
2 cloves garlic, minced	1 6-ounce can tomato
1/8 pound salt pork, diced	sauce
1 bay leaf	1 1/2 cups dry white wine
1/2 teaspoon thyme	1 tablespoon salt
2 tablespoons salad oil	2 garlic sausages
1 1/2 pounds pork, cubed	1 roast duck

Wash the beans, cover with water, and bring to a boil. Cook 2 minutes. Remove from heat and let soak 1 hour. Drain. Put in a deep pan with 2 quarts water, the onions stuck with the cloves, the garlic, salt pork, bay leaf, and thyme; bring to a boil, and cook over medium heat 1 hour.

Meanwhile, heat the oil in a skillet; brown the lamb and pork on all sides. Remove. Add the chopped onion to skillet and let brown. Mix browned meats, chopped onion, tomato sauce, wine, and salt into the pan of beans; cover, and cook over low heat 1 hour. Transfer to a large casserole. Slice the sausages and cut meat from bones of duck. Lightly mix them into the contents of casserole. Taste for seasoning, and bake in a 350° oven 40 minutes.

Serve with a red Bordeaux or Burgundy, a red Rhône wine, an Italian red wine like Bardolino or an American red wine.

Serves 8-10

ROAST LEG OF VEAL

1 leg of veal	2 carrots, diced
2 teaspoons salt	1/8 teaspoon thyme
1/2 teaspoon freshly ground black pepper	1 bay leaf
	1/2 cup melted butter
1 clove garlic, minced	1 cup dry white wine
2 onions, quartered	

Have the leg of veal boned, larded, and tied. Rub the veal with a mixture of the salt, pepper, and garlic.

Place the veal in a roasting pan, add the onions, carrots, thyme, and bay leaf. Roast in a 375° oven 20 minutes. Pour off the fat. Add the butter and wine. Reduce heat to 300° and roast 2 hours longer, or until meat is tender, basting frequently. (Or 170° on a meat thermometer). Transfer meat to a hot serving platter and skim the fat off the gravy.

Serve with any American red wine.

Serves 6-8

ROLLED VEAL RUMP WITH SOUR CREAM

4-pound boned rump of veal	2 teaspoons salt
2 cloves garlic, minced	1/2 teaspoon freshly ground black pepper
6 anchovies, mashed	
1/4 teaspoon thyme	2 tablespoons flour
6 tablespoons butter	1/4 cup dry sherry
2 cups dry white wine	1 cup sour cream
	2 tablespoons capers

Have the veal pounded lightly to flatten.

Lay the meat flat, with the boned surface up. Cream together the garlic, anchovies, thyme, and 2 tablespoons of butter. Spread over the meat, roll, and tie in several places. Place the veal in a glass or pottery bowl, pour the wine over it, and marinate 3 hours or more, turning and basting occasionally.

Drain and dry the meat, reserving the marinade. Rub the meat with the salt and pepper. Heat the remaining butter in a Dutch oven; brown the meat in it on all sides. Slip a rack under the meat, add the marinade, cover, and cook over low heat 2 hours, or until the meat is tender. Transfer the meat to a hot serving platter.

Blend the flour with the sherry, and stir into the gravy until thickened, then cook 2 minutes longer.

Blend in the sour cream and capers, taste for seasoning, and heat but do not let boil. Slice the meat, pour some of the gravy over it, and serve the rest separately.

Serve with any American red wine.

Serves 8

STUFFED VEAL CHOPS

6 rib veal chops, cut 3/4 inch thick	2 teaspoons salt
6 slices prosciutto ham	1/2 teaspoon freshly ground black pepper
6 tablespoons cream cheese	1/4 cup flour
1 tablespoon minced truffles	6 tablespoons butter
	3/4 cup dry white wine

Have the chops cut through center right to the bone. In each, put a slice of ham, a tablespoon of cream cheese and a few pieces of truffle. Press down the cut edges firmly and fasten with toothpicks. Season with the salt and pepper; dip in flour.

Heat the butter in a skillet; sauté the veal until browned on both sides. Add the wine; cover, and cook over low heat 20 minutes, or until tender, turning the chops once or twice.

Serve with any dry light red wine, especially a Bordeaux.

Serves 6

CÔTES DE VEAU AUX HERBES
(veal chops with herbes)

6 veal chops, cut 1 inch thick	1/4 cup chopped green onions
2 tablespoons olive oil	1 clove garlic, minced
6 tablespoons butter	1/2 teaspoon thyme
1 1/2 teaspoons salt	1/2 teaspoon basil
1/2 teaspoon freshly ground black pepper	1/2 cup dry white wine
	1/4 cup heavy cream

Rinse and dry the chops. Heat the oil and 2 tablespoons of the butter in a large skillet; brown the chops in it on both sides. Transfer to a shallow casserole and sprinkle with the salt and pepper. Pour off the fat from the skillet. Melt 2 tablespoons of the remaining butter in the skillet; sauté the green onions 2 minutes. Add the garlic, thyme, basil, and wine. Bring to a boil, scraping the skillet for any browned particles. Pour contents of skillet over the chops. Cover, and bake in a 325° oven 30 minutes, or until chops are tender. Baste, and turn a few times.

Transfer the chops to a hot plate. Place casserole over direct heat. Stir the cream into the pan juices. Bring to a boil, and cook over high heat 2 minutes. Taste for seasoning, then stir in the remaining butter in small pieces until just melted. Pour over the chops.

Serve with a light red Bordeaux or Burgundy, especially a Beaujolais, a rosé, or with an American red wine.

Serves 6

VITELLO CON PEPERONI
(veal and peppers)

4 tablespoons butter
3 pounds boneless veal, cut in 1/2-inch cubes
2 teaspoons salt
1/4 teaspoon dried ground red peppers
1/2 teaspoon oregano
2 tablespoons flour
1 cup beef broth

1 1/2 pounds tomatoes, chopped
1 cup Marsala wine or sweet sherry
4 tablespoons olive oil
1 1/2 cups thinly sliced onion
1 clove garlic, minced
4 green peppers, sliced

Melt the butter in a saucepan; sauté the veal, salt, red peppers, and oregano until browned, stirring frequently. Mix in the flour. Add the broth, tomatoes, and wine. Bring to a boil, cover, and cook over low heat 30 minutes, stirring occasionally.

Heat the oil in a skillet; sauté the onion slices, garlic, and green peppers 10 minutes, stirring occasionally. Then stir into the veal mixture. Cook 10 minutes longer. Taste for seasoning. Serve with macaroni or rice.

Serve with a dry Italian red wine like Bardolino, a red Bordeaux or Burgundy, a *rosé*, or an American red wine.

Serves 6-8

ESCALOPES DE VEAU À LA SAVOYARDE
(veal in vermouth sauce)

1 pound veal scaloppine	4 tablespoons butter
1/4 cup flour	1/2 cup dry vermouth
1 1/4 teaspoons salt	1/2 cup heavy cream
1/4 teaspoon white pepper	

You should have about 12 pieces of veal. Be sure the veal is cut thin, then pounded. Dip the pieces lightly in a mixture of the flour, salt, and pepper.

Melt the butter in a skillet; brown the veal in it over high heat. Add the vermouth, bring to a boil, and cook a few seconds. Add the cream, shaking the pan until the mixture boils, then cook over low heat 5 minutes, turning the veal once.

Serve with a dry white Burgundy, an Alsatian wine like Traminer, a dry German white wine, or a *rosé*.

Serves 4

OISEAX DE VEAU
(veal birds in wine)

2 pounds leg of veal	2 cloves garlic, minced
2 teaspoons salt	2 tablespoons minced parsley
1/2 teaspoon freshly ground black pepper	4 tablespoons butter
1/4 teaspoon nutmeg	1 cup dry white wine
1/4 teaspoon thyme	6 small white onions
1/4 pound sausage meat	1/2 pound mushrooms, sliced
1/2 teaspoon marjoram	1 bay leaf
3 tablespoons grated onion	

Have the butcher pound the veal as thin as possible; then cut into 6 pieces each, about 6 inches by 4 inches. Rub pieces with a mixture of 1 1/2 teaspoons salt, 1/4 teaspoon pepper, the nutmeg, and thyme.

Mix the sausage meat with the marjoram, grated onion, garlic, parsley, and remaining salt and pepper. Spread the mixture on the veal pieces and roll them up. Tie securely with bread, or fasten with skewers or toothpicks.

Melt the butter in a deep skillet; brown the veal rolls in it. Add the wine, onions, mushrooms, and bay leaf. Cover, and bake in a 375° oven 45 minutes, or until tender. Shake the casserole once or twice, but don't lift the cover. Discard the bay leaf, and taste for seasoning.

Serve with a red Bordeaux or Burgundy, a dry white Burgundy, a dry German white wine, or an American red or white wine.

Serves 6

VEAL STEW IN RED WINE

1/4 pound salt pork, diced	3 tablespoons flour
3 pounds boneless veal, cut in 1 1/2-inch cubes	2 cups dry red wine
	2 teaspoons finely chopped bay leaves
12 small white onions	1/4 teaspoon thyme
3 carrots, sliced	1/2 pound mushrooms, sliced and sautéed
1 1/2 teaspoons salt	
1/2 teaspoon white pepper	2 tablespoons minced parsley
1 clove garlic, minced	

Brown the salt pork in a deep skillet or casserole; remove the browned pieces and reserve. Pour off all but 3 tablespoons fat. In the fat remaining, brown the veal, onions, and carrots. Sprinkle with the salt, pepper, garlic, and flour; add the wine, bay leaves, and thyme. Cover, and cook over low heat 1 1/4 hours, or until the veal is tender. Skim off the fat. Add the pork bits, mushrooms, and parsley. Cook 5 minutes longer. Taste for seasoning.

Serve with a dry red Bordeaux or Burgundy, an Italian red wine like Bardolino, a *rosé*, or an American red wine.

Serves 6-8

FRENCH VEAL AND BLACK OLIVES

3 pounds boneless veal,
    cut into 1 1/2-inch
    cubes
1/2 cup flour
2 1/2 teaspoons salt
1/2 teaspoon freshly
    ground black pepper
4 tablespoons butter

3/4 cup sliced onion
1 clove garlic, minced
1/2 teaspoon thyme
1 cup dry white wine
1 tablespoon tomato paste
1/2 cup chicken broth
1 cup sliced black olives

Toss the veal in a mixture of the flour, salt, and pepper.
Melt the butter in a casserole or deep skillet with ovenproof handle; brown the veal in it. Mix in the sliced onion
and garlic; cook until onions brown. Add the thyme, wine,
tomato paste, and broth. Cover, and bake in a 325° oven
2 hours. Add the olives, and bake 15 minutes longer.

Serve with a white Burgundy, a dry German white wine,
an Alsatian wine like Traminer, or a *rosé*.

Serves 6-8

FRICADELLES DE VEAU À LA CRÈME
(veal croquettes with cream)

3 slices white bread,
    trimmed
1/2 cup milk
1 pound ground veal
1 1/4 teaspoons salt
1/2 teaspoon white
    pepper
1 egg, beaten

1/4 cup minced parsley
1/2 cup flour
3 tablespoons vegetable
    oil
4 tablespoons butter
1/2 cup dry white wine
1 teaspoon basil
1/2 cup heavy cream

Soak the bread in the milk until very soft, then drain
and mash smooth. Mix with the veal, salt, pepper, egg,
and 3 tablespoons of the parsley. Shape into 8 patties, 1/2
inch thick. Dip in the flour.

Heat the oil and 2 tablespoons of the butter in a large
skillet. Brown the patties in it on both sides. Pour off most
of the fat, cover the skillet, and cook over low heat 15
minutes, turning the patties once.

Transfer patties to a hot serving platter. Pour off the fat. Add the wine and basil. Bring to a boil, scraping the bottom for any browned particles. Add the cream; cook over high heat 3 minutes. Stir in the remaining butter in small pieces until melted. Pour over the patties, and sprinkle them with the remaining parsley.

Serve with a light red Burgundy or Bordeaux, a white Burgundy, a *rosé*, or an American red wine.

Serves 4-6

MOUSSE AU JAMBON
(ham mousse)

1 envelop (tablespoon) gelatin	1/8 teaspoon cayenne pepper
1/4 cup cold water	2 cups finely ground
1 1/2 cups beef broth	boiled ham
1 cup medium sherry	3/4 cup heavy cream
1/2 teaspoon salt	

Soften the gelatin in the water. Bring the broth to a boil; stir in the gelatin until dissolved. Mix in the sherry, salt, and cayenne pepper. Cool until mixture begins to thicken, then beat with an electric mixer or rotary beater until foamy. Mix in the ham, and taste for seasoning.

Whip the cream, and fold into the ham mixture. Turn into a lightly oiled 1 1/2-quart mold. Chill until set. Carefully unmold onto a chilled serving dish.

Serve with a *rosé* wine.

Serves 4-6

TRANCHES DE JAMBON AUX MADÈRE
(sautéed sliced ham in Madeira)

6 slices cooked ham, cut 1/2-inch thick	3/4 cup beef broth
3 tablespoons butter	2 teaspoons tomato paste
3 tablespoons chopped green onions	1/8 teaspoon freshly ground black pepper
3 tablespoons flour	1 1/4 cups heavy cream
3/4 cup Madeira or sweet sherry	3 tablespoons cognac

Trim the fat off the ham. Cut each slice in half cross-wise. Melt the butter in a skillet; brown the ham in it on both sides. Remove ham and keep it warm. Pour off all but 2 tablespoons of the fat. Add the chopped green onions; sauté 1 minute. Blend in the flour; cook 1 minute. Gradually add the wine and broth, stirring steadily to the boiling point. Blend in the tomato paste and pepper; cook over low heat 5 minutes. Stir in the cream, bring to a boil, and cook over low heat 5 minutes. Return ham to the skillet; cook 5 minutes, basting frequently. Heat cognac; set aflame and pour over the ham.

Serve with a dry American or German white wine, a white Burgundy, a dry Italian white wine like white Chianti, or a rosé.

Serves 6

JAMBON À LA CRÈME
(ham in cream sauce)

3 tablespoons butter
6 slices boiled ham, cut
    1/2 inch thick

1 tablespoon flour
1 cup dry white wine
1/2 cup heavy cream

Melt the butter in a skillet. Cook the ham over low heat for 2 minutes on each side. Sprinkle with the flour. Stir in the wine. Cook over medium heat until the liquid is reduced to about half. Transfer the ham to a hot platter. Stir the cream into the pan juices. Bring to a boil, and immediately pour over the ham.

Serve with a dry American or German white wine, a white Burgundy, or a rosé.

Serves 6

MAIALE MARINATO
(marinated fresh ham)

5 pounds fresh ham
3 cups dry red wine
1 cup chopped onion
1/2 cup sliced carrot
2 cloves garlic, minced
1/4 teaspoon thyme
1 bay leaf
2 teaspoons salt

1/2 teaspoon freshly
    ground black pepper
2 tablespoons olive oil
1 cup beef broth
2 tablespoons minced
    parsley
3 tablespoons capers

Trim the fat off the ham, and place ham in a glass or pottery bowl. Mix together the wine, onion, carrot, garlic, thyme, bay leaf, salt, and pepper. Pour over the ham; marinate overnight, basting occasionally. Drain the meat, reserving the marinade.

Heat the oil in a Dutch oven; brown the meat in it. Pour off the fat. Heat the marinade and pour over the meat. Cover and roast in a 350° oven 3 hours, or until tender. Add a little of the broth from time to time and baste frequently. Transfer the meat to a platter. Skim the fat from the gravy and stir in the parsley and capers.

Serve with a German or American white wine, or if you wish, with a *rosé*.

Serves 8-10

JAMBON AU ANANAS
(ham with champagne sauce and pineapple)

12-pound ham
2 beaten eggs
1 cup brown sugar
1 can sliced pineapple

1 1/2 cups champagne or
    dry white wine
2 tablespoons butter

Cook the ham according to the package directions, and drain well. Score the fat in a diamond design, brush with the egg, and spread with the brown sugar. Drain the pineapple and reserve 3/4 cup juice. Put ham in a roasting pan and pour the pineapple juice and champagne around it. Bake in a 375° oven 1 hour, basting frequently to glaze. Transfer ham to a hot serving platter. Skim the fat from the pan juices.

Melt the butter in a skillet, and lightly brown the pineapple slices on both sides. Arrange around the ham. Serve the gravy separately.

Serve with champagne, a dry American or German white wine, a white Burgundy like Pouilly-Fuissé, or a dry Italian white wine like Orvieto.

Serves 12-16

MARINATED PORK LOIN

8-pound loin of pork
1 quart dry red wine
1 tablespoon wine vinegar
1 cup chopped onions
2 cloves garlic, minced
2 teaspoons salt
3/4 teaspoon freshly
    ground black pepper

1/2 teaspoon thyme
2 bay leaves
2 tablespoons lard or
    butter
1/4 cup orange
    marmalade

Have the pork boned and tied up.

Combine the wine, vinegar, chopped onion, garlic, salt, pepper, thyme, and bay leaves in a saucepan. Bring to a boil, and cook over low heat 10 minutes. Place the pork in a large glass or pottery bowl and pour the marinade over it. Marinate in the refrigerator 24-36 hours, turning the meat and basting occasionally. Remove meat, dry with paper towels, and reserve the marinade.

Heat the fat in a Dutch oven or casserole; brown the meat in it on all sides. Pour off the fat. Heat the marinade and pour half over the meat. Cover, and roast in a 350° oven 2 1/2 hours, or until tender, basting frequently and adding more marinade as needed. Remove cover for last half-hour.

Transfer the meat to a platter. Strain the gravy into a saucepan and skim off the fat. Stir the marmalade into it, and taste for seasoning. Thicken, if necessary, with a little cornstarch or flour mixed with water.

Serve with a *rosé* wine.

Serves 6-8

ASADO DE PUERCO
(marinated roast pork)

8-pound loin of pork
2 1/2 teaspoons salt
1 teaspoon freshly
    ground black pepper
3 cloves garlic, minced
1/2 teaspoon oregano

2 cups chopped onion
2 1/2 cups dry red wine
3 tablespoons olive oil
1 1/2 tablespoons
    cornstarch

Rub the pork with a mixture of the salt, pepper, garlic, and oregano. Place in a large glass or pottery bowl with the chopped onion and 1 1/2 cups wine. Marinate in the refrigerator overnight, basting occasionally.

Heat the oil in a roasting pan. Put the undrained pork into it. Roast in a 350° oven 3 hours, basting frequently. Pour off the gravy into a saucepan and skim off the fat. Mix the cornstarch with the remaining wine, and stir into the gravy. Cook over low heat, stirring constantly, until thickened; then cook 5 minutes longer.

Serve with a *rosé* wine.

Serves 8-10

PUERCO HORNEADO
(spiced roast pork)

3 cloves garlic, minced	1/2 cup boiling water
2 1/2 teaspoons salt	1 cup dry white wine
1 teaspoon freshly ground black pepper	1/4 cup grated onion
1/2 teaspoon saffron	2 tablespoons wine vinegar
1/2 teaspoon ground cumin	3 tablespoons minced parsley
1/2 teaspoon marjoram	1/4 teaspoon dried ground chili peppers
6-pound loin of pork	

Pound together the garlic, salt, pepper, saffron, cumin, and marjoram; rub into the pork. Wrap in waxed paper or foil, and refrigerate overnight.

Place the pork in a shallow roasting pan. Roast in a 425° oven 25 minutes. Pour off the fat. Reduce heat to 350°, pour the water and 1/2 cup of the wine over the pork, and roast 2 hours longer, basting frequently. Transfer pork to a platter; skim the fat from the pan and place pan over direct heat. Mix in the grated onion, vinegar, parsley, chili peppers, and remaining wine; bring to a boil, scraping the bottom of the pan for browned particles. Cook 2 minutes, and serve in a sauceboat.

Serve with a white Burgundy, a dry American or Italian white wine, or a *rosé*.

Serves 4-6

RÔTI DE PORC PROVENÇALE
(roast pork with parsley coating)

8-rib loin of pork	2 cups dry white wine
2 cloves garlic, slivered	1/2 teaspoon thyme
2 teaspoons salt	1/4 cup dry bread crumbs
1/2 teaspoon freshly ground black pepper	1/2 cup chopped parsley

Have the butcher saw the bottom of bones at 1/4-inch intervals. Insert a garlic sliver in each. Rub the pork with the salt and pepper. Place in a large glass or pottery bowl and pour the wine, mixed with the thyme, over it. Let marinate at room temperature 2 hours, basting and turning the meat several times.

Put the pork in a roasting pan, fat side up, and pour 1 cup of marinade over it. Cover the pan with a piece of oiled aluminum foil, and roast in a 350° oven 1 hour.

Mix together the bread crumbs and parsley. Remove the foil from the pan and spread the parsley mixture over the top of the pork, pressing it in. Pour the remaining marinade into the pan. Reduce heat to 325° and roast pork 1 hour longer, basting frequently.

Serve with a dry American or German white wine, a dry white Burgundy, a white Rhône wine like Hermitage Blanc, or a *rosé*.

Serves 4-6

LOMO CON JEREZ
(loin pork with sherry)

4-pound loin of pork	2 tablespoons minced parsley
2 1/2 teaspoons salt	2 tablespoons olive oil
1/2 teaspoon freshly ground black pepper	2 cups medium sherry
2 cloves garlic, minced	

Have the fat trimmed and the loin tied up. Rub with a mixture of the salt, pepper, garlic, and parsley. Let stand 2 hours.

Heat the oil in a deep skillet or Dutch oven. Brown the pork in it on all sides. Pour off the fat. Add the sherry;

bake in a 350° oven 1 3/4 hours, or until the pork is tender. Baste frequently.

Serve with a *rosé* wine.

Serves 4-6

BRACIOLINE DI MAIALE AL VINO
(pork chops in wine)

6 pork chops, cut 1 inch thick
1 1/2 teaspoons salt
1/2 teaspoon black pepper
1/4 cup flour
3 teaspoons olive oil

1/2 cup dry red wine
1/4 cup Marsala or sweet sherry
1 clove garlic, minced
1/4 cup water
1 tablespoon tomato paste

Trim the fat off the chops, and pound them slightly to flatten. Dip in a mixture of the salt, pepper, and flour. Heat the oil in a skillet; brown the chops in it, then cover skillet and cook over low heat 10 minutes on each side. Pour off the fat. Stir the wines into the skillet; cook over high heat until liquid is reduced to half. Mix in the garlic, water, and tomato paste; cook over low heat 20 minutes longer.

Serve with any dry American or Italian red wine.

Serves 6

PORK CHOPS PIZZAIOLA

6 pork chops, cut 1 inch thick
2 teaspoons salt
1/2 teaspoon freshly ground black pepper
2 cloves garlic, minced
2 tablespoons olive oil
1/2 cup canned tomato sauce

1/2 cup dry red wine
1/4 teaspoon oregano
2 green peppers, cut julienne
1/2 pound mushrooms, sliced
3 Italian sausages, sliced

Trim the fat off the chops and rub chops with a mixture of the salt, pepper, and garlic. Let stand 15 minutes. Heat the oil in a skillet; brown the chops on both sides. Add the tomato sauce, wine, oregano, green peppers and mushrooms. Cover, and cook over low heat 25 minutes, or until chops are tender.

Brown the sausages in another pan, drain, and add to skillet. Cook 10 minutes longer. Taste for seasoning.

Serve with Beaujolais, a dry American or Italian red wine, or a *rosé*.

Serves 6

CÔTES DE PORC AUX PRUNEAUX
(pork chops with prunes)

18 unsweetened prunes	1/4 cup flour
1 cup port	2 tablespoons butter
6 pork chops, 1 inch thick	2 tablespoons cognac
1 1/2 teaspoons salt	2 tablespoons heavy cream
1/4 teaspoon freshly	
ground black pepper	

Soak the prunes in hot water 15 minutes. Drain. Add the port and cook 15 minutes, or until tender but firm.

Season the chops with the salt and pepper, and dust with the flour. Melt the butter in a skillet and sauté the chops 30 minutes, or until browned and no pink remains. Transfer the chops to a hot serving platter.

Drain the prunes, reserving 1/2 cup liquid, and arrange them around the chops. Heat the cognac and pour into the skillet; set aflame. When flames die, add the prune liquid and cream; cook over high heat 1 minute, scraping bottom of pan for browned particles. Pour over the chops.

Serve with a dry American or German white wine, a white Burgundy, or a *rosé*.

Serves 6

PORK CHOPS WITH OLIVES

6 pork chops, cut 1 inch thick	1 cup sliced onion
	2 cloves garlic, minced
1/3 cup flour	2 cups chopped tomatoes
2 1/2 teaspoons salt	3/4 cup dry white wine
3/4 teaspoon freshly ground black pepper	2 hard-cooked eggs, chopped
2 tablespoons olive oil	1/2 cup sliced black olives

Trim the fat off the chops; dip in a mixture of the flour, 1 1/2 teaspoons of the salt, and 1/2 teaspoon pepper. Heat the oil in a skillet; brown the chops in it. Remove the chops. In the oil remaining in the skillet, sauté the onion slices and garlic 10 minutes. Add the tomatoes and remaining salt and pepper. Cook over low heat 10 minutes. Stir in the wine, and return the chops to skillet. Baste a few times. Cover, and bake in a 375° oven 45 minutes, or until the chops are tender. Remove cover for last 10 minutes. Sprinkle with the eggs and olives.

Serve with a dry American or German white wine, a white Burgundy, any dry Italian white wine like Soave, or a *rosé*.

Serves 6

PORK CHOPS AND APPLES

6 pork chops, cut 1 inch thick	12 small white onions
1 1/2 teaspoons salt	1/4 cup seedless raisins
1/4 teaspoon freshly ground black pepper	1 cup dry white wine
	2 tablespoons sweet sherry
4 apples, peeled and quartered	3 tablespoons brown sugar
	1/8 teaspoon thyme
	1/4 teaspoon nutmeg

Season the chops with the salt and pepper. Brown the chops for 5 minutes on each side, and drain. Arrange in a casserole or baking dish with the apples, onions, and raisins over them. Add the white wine, sherry, brown sugar, thyme, and nutmeg. Cover, and bake in a 375° oven 1 1/4 hours, removing the cover for the last 15 minutes. Taste for seasoning.

Serve with a dry American or German white wine, or a white Burgundy.

Serves 6

SPEZZATO DI MAIALE
(minced pork and onions)

3 tablespoons butter	1/4 teaspoon freshly ground black pepper
4 cups chopped onion	
1 1/2 teaspoons salt	1 cup dry white wine
2 pounds pork, cut in 1/8-inch dice	1 tablespoon flour
	3/4 cup beef broth

Melt 2 tablespoons of the butter in a skillet; mix in the chopped onion and half the salt. Cook over low heat 20 minutes, stirring frequently. Spread half the chopped onion on the bottom of a baking dish. Season the pork with the pepper and remaining salt. Spread over the onion, and cover with the remaining onion. Pour the wine into the dish.

Melt the remaining butter in a saucepan; blend in the flour. Gradually add the broth, stirring steadily to the boiling point. Cook over low heat 5 minutes, then pour over the onion. Bake in a 350° oven 1 1/4 hours. Serve with boiled potatoes.

Serve with a dry American or German white wine, or a chilled *rosé*.

Serves 4-6

RÔTI DE PORC PÔELÉ
(roast pork casserole)

4-pound boned rolled loin of pork	8 peppercorns
1 tablespoon salt	1 teaspoon thyme
1/2 cup wine vinegar	2 bay leaves
1 cup dry white wine	3 tablespoons vegetable oil
1/4 cup olive oil	1/2 cup sliced green onions
2 cloves garlic, split	
1/2 cup sliced onion	1/2 cup beef broth
1/2 cup sliced carrot	

Have the pork tied. Rub the meat with the salt. In a glass or pottery bowl, combine the vinegar, wine, olive oil, garlic, onion, carrot, peppercorns thyme and bay leaves. Marinate the pork in the mixture 24-36 hours in the refrigerator basting and turning the meat frequently. Drain the meat, and dry with paper towels.

Heat the vegetable oil in a casserole; brown the pork in it on all sides. Pour off all but 2 tablespoons of the fat. Add the green onions; cover, and bake in a 325° oven 2 1/4 hours, basting and turning meat a few times.

Transfer meat to a hot serving platter. Place casserole over direct low heat. Add the broth to the casserole; bring to a boil, and cook over high heat 3 minutes. Skim off the fat, and serve broth in a sauceboat.

Serve with a dry American or German white wine, a

white Rhône wine like Hermitage Blanc, a white Burgundy, or a *rosé*.

Serves 8

CHOUCROUTE À L'ALSACIENNE
(sauerkraut casserole)

4 slices salt pork
2 cloves
1 onion
2 pounds sauerkraut
2 cloves garlic, minced
1/2 teaspoon freshly
ground black pepper

3 cups dry white wine
6 pork chops
1 1/2 teaspoons salt
6 knockwurst (thick
frankfurters)

Cook the salt pork in boiling water 10 minutes. Drain well and dry. Place the salt pork on the bottom of a casserole. Stick the cloves in the onion and add to the casserole with the sauerkraut, garlic, pepper, and wine. Cover, and cook over low heat 2 hours. Brown the pork chops in a skillet; season with the salt, and add to the sauerkraut. Recover, and cook 1 hour. Add the knockwurst; cook 15 minutes longer.

Serves 6

TOURTE LORRAINE
(meat pie, Lorraine style)

1 clove garlic, minced
1/4 cup chopped onion
1 tablespoon chopped
parsley
1 cup dry white wine
1 3/4 teaspoons salt
1/4 teaspoon freshly
ground black pepper

1 pound lean pork, cut
in 1/2-inch dice
1 pound veal, cut in
1/2-inch dice
Pastry for 2-crust pie
3 eggs, beaten
2 cups cream

In a glass or pottery bowl, mix together the garlic, onion, parsley, wine, 1 1/2 teaspoons of the salt, and pepper; marinate the pork and veal in the mixture 24 hours in the refrigerator. Line an 11-inch, deep pie plate with half the pastry. Drain the meats and dry well, then put in the lined pie plate. Cover with the remaining pastry, and seal the edges. Cut a small hole in the center of the pastry. Bake the pie in a preheated 425° oven 25 minutes.

Beat together the eggs, cream, and remaining salt. Insert a small funnel in the hole in the pie crust and pour in the egg-cream mixture very slowly. Reduce heat to 325°, and bake 20 minutes longer. Serve hot.

Serve with a red Burgundy or Bordeaux, or a red American wine.

Serves 6-8

PORK SAUSAGES IN WINE

6 pork chops, cut 1 inch thick
1 1/2 teaspoons salt
1/2 teaspoon freshly ground black pepper
3 slices bacon, cut in small pieces
1 cup thinly sliced onion

1 cup diced carrots
1 tablespoon flour
1 1/2 cups dry white wine
1 bay leaf
1/2 pound spicy sausages, sliced (Italian or Spanish)

Season the pork chops with the salt and pepper. Lightly brown the bacon in a deep skillet; pour off the fat. Add the onion slices and carrots; sauté 5 minutes. Arrange the chops in the pan; brown lightly on both sides. Sprinkle with the flour, and add the wine and bay leaf; cover, and cook over low heat 45 minutes. Add the sausages, re-cover, and cook 30 minutes longer, or until the pork is tender. Skim off the fat.

Serve with a dry American or German white wine, a white Burgundy, or a *rosé*.

Serves 6

HAWAIIAN–CHINESE SPARERIBS

1/2 cup soy sauce
1/2 cup ketchup
1/2 cup dry sherry
3/4 cup brown sugar
1 teaspoon salt

1 clove garlic, minced
1/2-inch piece ginger root, crushed, or 1 teaspoon powdered ginger
1 rack of spareribs

Mix the soy sauce, ketchup, sherry, sugar, salt, garlic, and ginger. Rub into the spareribs very well, then let spareribs marinate for 3 hours. Remove spareribs and place on a rack, with a shallow pan under it. Cover the bottom of the pan with 1/2 inch of water. Roast in a 350° oven 45 minutes, or until spareribs are browned and tender. Baste with marinade, and turn spareribs frequently. Cut into individual ribs, and serve with Chinese mustard and Chinese *duk* sauce for dunking.

Serves 6-8 as an appetizer or first course.

GLAZED TONGUE CASSEROLE

5-pound fresh beef tongue	3 cups dry white wine
2 cloves	3 tablespoons honey
1 onion	1 teaspoon cinnamon
1 bay leaf	4 thin slices lemon
6 peppercorns	

Wash the tongue, and place in a saucepan with water to cover. Add the cloves, onion, bay leaf, and peppercorns. Bring to a boil, cover, and cook over low heat 3 hours. Drain, and cool 30 minutes. Peel off the skin, and cut away the roots. Cut the tongue in 1/4-inch slices.

Arrange the sliced tongue in a casserole; add a mixture of the wine, honey, cinnamon, and lemon slices. Cover, and bake in a 375° oven 30 minutes, or until liquid is almost absorbed.

Serve with a red Bordeaux, a red Rhône wine, or a dry red American wine.

Serves 6-8

TONGUE WITH MUSHROOM–WINE SAUCE

5-pound smoked tongue	2 tablespoons flour
2 cloves garlic, minced	1 1/2 cups dry red wine
3 tablespoons butter	1 tablespoon minced
3/4 cup chopped onion	parsley
2 cups chopped mushrooms	

Wash the tongue, cover with water, and bring to a boil. Drain; then add fresh boiling water to cover, and the garlic. Cover, and cook over low heat 2 1/2 hours, or until tongue is tender. Drain, reserving 1 1/2 cups stock. Remove the skin, and cut away the roots of the tongue.

Melt the butter in a saucepan; sauté the onion 5 minutes. Add the mushrooms; sauté 5 minutes. Blend in the flour until browned. Gradually add the wine and the reserved stock, stirring steadily to the boiling point. Cook over low heat 10 minutes. Stir in the parsley. Slice the tongue, and serve with the sauce.

Serve with a red Bordeaux, a red Rhône like Hermitage or Châteauneuf-du-Pape, or a red American wine.

Serves 8-10

TONGUE IN OLIVE SAUCE

5-pound pickled tongue	3 tablespoons lemon juice
1 onion	2 teaspoons sugar
1 stalk celery	1/2 teaspoon freshly
3 tablespoons butter	ground black pepper
1 cup chopped onion	1/2 teaspoon powdered
1 clove garlic, minced	ginger
2 tablespoons flour	1 teaspoon finely chopped
1 cup dry white wine	bay leaf
1/2 cup canned tomato	1 cup sliced black olives
sauce	

Cook the tongue, the onion, and celery in water to cover, 3 hours, or until tender, adding boiling water from time to time to keep covered. Drain, reserving 1 cup stock. Skin the tongue, and remove roots.

Melt the butter in a saucepan; sauté the chopped onion and garlic 10 minutes. Blend in the flour until browned; gradually add the combined stock, wine, and tomato sauce, stirring constantly to the boiling point. Mix in the lemon juice, sugar, pepper, ginger, bay leaf, and olives. Cook over low heat 5 minutes. Slice the tongue, and heat in the sauce for 10 minutes. Taste for seasoning.

Serve with a red Rhône wine like Châteauneuf-du-Pape, a light red Bordeaux, or a red American wine.

Serves 8-10

CASSEROLE OF VENISON

3 pounds venison, cut
    into 1 1/2-inch cubes
1/4 cup flour
2 teaspoons salt
1/4 teaspoon freshly
    ground black pepper
3 tablespoons vegetable
    oil

1 cup chopped onion
2 cloves garlic, minced
1 teaspoon paprika
2 cups dry red wine
1/2 cup water
1 tablespoon tomato paste
1 cup sour cream

Toss the venison in a mixture of the flour, salt, and pepper. Heat the oil in a cassrole; brown the meat in it. Add the onion and garlic; cook 10 minutes, stirring frequently. Blend in the paprika, then the wine, water, and tomato paste. Bring to a boil, cover, and cook over low heat 2 1/2 hours, or until meat is tender. Watch carefully, and add a little boiling water if necessary. Just before serving, stir the sour cream into the gravy. Heat, but do not let boil.

Serve with a red Burgundy, a red Rhône wine like Hermitage, or an Italian red wine like Bardolino.

Serves 6-8

SAUSAGE–MEAT LOAF

3/4 pound sausage meat
1 1/2 pounds ground beef
2 tablespoons grated onion
1 clove garlic, minced
2 eggs beaten
1 1/2 teaspoons salt
1/2 teaspoon freshly
    ground black pepper

1/2 teaspoon oregano
2 tablespoons minced
    parsley
1/4 cup flour
1 cup dry red wine

Mix the sausage meat with the other ingedients except the flour and wine. Shape into a loaf, and sprinkle with the flour; place in a greased pan. Add the wine. Bake in a 350° oven 1 hour, basting frequently. Serve hot or cold.

Serve with a red Bordeaux or Burgundy, or a red American wine.

Serves 8-10

FOIE DE VEAU AU VIN ROUGE
(calf's liver in red wine)

4 tablespoon's butter	1 1/2 teaspoons salt
2 1/2 pounds calf's liver (one piece)	1/4 teaspoon freshly ground black pepper
1 cup sliced onion	2 tablespoons minced parsley
2 carrots, sliced	
1 clove garlic, minced	2 cups dry red wine
1 bay leaf	1 cup beef broth
1/2 teaspoon thyme	2 tablespoons flour

Melt the butter in a casserole; brown the liver in it on both sides. Add the sliced onion, carrots, and garlic; sauté until lightly browned. Add the bay leaf, thyme, salt, pepper, parsley, 1 3/4 cups wine, and the broth. Cover, and bake in a 375° oven 2 hours. Turn liver occasionally. Place casserole over direct heat; mix the flour and remaining wine together, and stir into gravy until thickened. Cook over low heat 10 minutes. Slice the liver and serve with the gravy.

Serve with a dry red Bordeaux or Burgundy, especially a Beaujolais, a dry Italian red wine like Barolo, or a dry American red wine.

Serves 6-8

FEGATO DI VITELLO AL MARSALA
(calf's liver in Marsala)

1 pound calf's liver, sliced 1/8 inch thick	1/4 teaspoon white pepper
2 tablespoons lemon juice	4 tablespoons butter
1/3 cup flour	1/3 cup Marsala or sweet sherry
1 1/4 teaspoons salt	

Wash and dry the liver; rub with the lemon juice, then dip in the flour mixed with the salt and pepper. Melt the

butter in a skillet; fry the liver over high heat 1 minute
on each side. Stir the wine into the pan; cook over low
heat 2 minutes, basting almost constantly.

Serve with a dry red Bordeaux or Burgundy, especially
a Beaujolais, a dry Italian red wine like Valpolicella, or a
dry red American wine.

Serves 4

FEGATO DI VITELLO ALLA VENEZIANA
(calf's liver, with onions and wine)

1 pound calf's liver
1/4 pound butter
1 1/2 cups thinly sliced
    onion
1 teaspoon salt

1/4 teaspoon freshly
    ground black pepper
1/4 cup dry white wine
2 tablespoons minced
    parsley

Cut the liver in paper-thin slices, and then into strips about
1 inch by 2 inches.

Melt the butter in a skillet; add the onion slices. Cover,
and cook the onions over very low heat 15 minutes, or
until lightly browned and soft. Add the liver, and cook
over high heat 3 minutes, stirring almost constantly. Season with the salt and pepper. Transfer to a hot platter. Stir
the wine and parsley into the skillet; bring to a boil and
pour over the liver.

Serve with a dry red Bordeaux or Burgundy, a dry Italian
red wine like Valpolicella, or a dry red American wine.

Serves 4

RIS DE VEAU LUCULLUS
(creamed sweetbreads and mushrooms, Lucullus)

3 pairs parboiled
    sweetbreads
6 tablespoons butter
1 cup port
1 pound mushrooms,
    sliced

2 teaspoons beef extract
1 teaspoon salt
1/4 teaspoon freshly
    ground white pepper
2 cups heavy cream

Cut the parboiled sweetbreads in four. Heat 4 tablespoons butter in a casserole; lightly brown the sweetbreads in it. Add the port; cook over low heat until reduced to half. Melt the remaining butter in a skillet; sauté the mushrooms 5 minutes. Mix into casserole with the beef extract, salt, pepper, and cream. Cover, and bake in a 350° oven 20 minutes. Thicken sauce, if necessary, with 1 tablespoon flour kneaded with 1 tablespoon butter.

Serve with a white Burgundy or Bordeaux, a dry German white wine, or a dry white American wine.

Serves 6

SAUTÉED SWEETBREADS WITH MUSHROOMS

2 pair parboiled
    sweetbreads
1/4 cup flour
3 tablespoons butter
1 teaspoon salt
1/4 teaspoon white pepper
2 tablespoons warmed
    cognac

3/4 cup dry white wine
1/4 cup chicken broth
1/2 teaspoon tomato paste
1 clove garlic, minced
8 mushroom caps,
    sautéed
2 tablespoons minced
    parsley

Cut the sweetbreads in half lengthwise, so as to make them half as thick. Dip them in the flour (reserve 1 tablespoon). Melt the butter in a skillet; brown the sweetbreads on both sides. Season with the salt and pepper. Pour the warmed cognac over them and set aflame. Remove sweetbreads from skillet and keep warm. Blend the reserved flour into the pan. Add the wine, broth, tomato paste, and garlic, stirring steadily to the boiling point; cook over low heat 5 minutes. Place the sweetbreads on toast or sautéed bread slices, with a mushroom on top of each. Pour the sauce over all, and sprinkle with the parsley.

Serve with a dry white Burgundy, a dry German or American white wine, or an Italian white wine like Orvieto or white Chianti.

Serves 8, as a first course, or 4 as a main course.

RIS DE VEAU AU VIN BLANC
(sweetbreads in white wine)

4 pair sweetbreads
1 tablespoon vinegar
3 cups water
3 tablespoons butter
1 1/2 cups sliced onion
1 cup grated carrot
3 tablespoons minced
  parsley
1 bay leaf
1 1/2 teaspoons salt

1/4 teaspoon white
  pepper
2 tablespoons sweet
  sherry
1 cup dry white wine
1/2 cup chicken broth
2 cups fresh or frozen
  green peas
3/4 cup chopped
  mushrooms

Wash the sweetbreads and soak in ice water for 2 hours; drain, and combine in a saucepan with the vinegar and water. Bring to a boil, and cook over low heat 10 minutes. Drain, cover with cold water, and let cool. Drain. Remove membranes and tubes, and cut each sweetbread in quarters.

Melt the butter in a casserole; sauté the onion slices and grated carrot for 10 minutes, stirring frequently. Arrange the sweetbreads over them and add the parsley, bay leaf, salt, pepper, sherry, white wine, broth, peas, and mushrooms. Bake in a 375° oven 1 hour, turning the sweetbreads once or twice. Discard bay leaf.

Serve with a white Burgundy, a dry German or American white wine, or a Loire Valley white wine like Pouilly-Fumé.

Serves 6-8

SWEETBREADS, HAM, AND MUSHROOMS

3 pair sweetbreads
1 tablespoon vinegar
2 teaspoons salt
1/4 cup flour
4 tablespoons olive oil
4 tablespoons butter

1/4 teaspoon white
  pepper
1 cup sliced sautéed
  mushrooms
1/2 cup julienne-cut
  cooked ham
3/4 cup dry white wine

Wash the sweetbreads, cover with cold water, and let soak 1 hour. Drain, add fresh water to cover, the vinegar, and 1 teaspoon salt. Bring to a boil, and cook over low heat 5 minutes. Drain, cover with cold water, and let stand 20 minutes. Drain, remove the membranes and tubes, but leave the sweetbreads whole. Dry, then dip lightly in the flour.

Heat the oil in a skillet; brown the sweetbreads in it. Pour off the oil. Add the butter, pepper, mushrooms, ham, wine, and the remaining salt. Bring to a boil and cook over low heat 10 minutes.

Serve with a white Burgundy, a dry German or American white wine, or a dry white Bordeaux.

Serves 6

RIS DE VEAU AU MARRONS
(sweetbreads with chestnuts and mushrooms)

6 pair sweetbreads	1/2 cup Madeira wine
1 tablespoon vinegar	3/4 cup chicken broth
2 teaspoons salt	1/4 teaspoon freshly
6 tablespoons butter	ground black pepper
1 cup chopped onion	1/2 cup diced ham
3/4 cup grated carrot	3/4 cup sliced mushrooms
1/2 cup chopped celery	1/2 cup coarsely chopped
1/2 cup dry white wine	cooked chestnuts

Soak the sweetbreads in cold water for 2 hours in the refrigerator. Drain, and cover with fresh water. Add the vinegar and salt. Bring to a boil, and cook 5 minutes. Drain, and remove the membranes. Place a weight on the sweetbreads (a breadboard or a plate) and chill.

Melt 3 tablespoons butter in a skillet; sauté the onion, carrot, and celery for 10 minutes. Add the white wine and Madeira. Arrange the sweetbreads in the skillet and add enough of the broth to half cover them. Season with the pepper. Cover, and bake in a 350° oven 30 minutes.

In a separate skillet, melt remaining butter. Sauté the

ham, mushrooms, and chestnuts in it for 5 minutes. Add
to the sweetbreads, and taste for seasoning.

Serve with a dry red American wine.

Serves 6

QUEUE DE BOEUF
(braised oxtails in red wine)

2 oxtails	3 cups dry red wine
1/2 cup flour	3 cups water
3 slices salt pork, diced	2 teaspoons tomato paste
1 cup diced onion	3 potatoes, peeled and
1 carrot, grated	quartered
1 teaspoon salt	2 cups fresh or frozen
1/2 teaspoon freshly	green peas
ground black pepper	

Have the oxtails cut in 1-inch pieces. Cover with boiling
water, drain, and dry. Roll in the flour. Brown the salt
pork in a Dutch oven or casserole; drain off all but 2 tablespoons fat. Add the oxtails, onion, and grated carrot, and
cook until browned. Mix in the salt, pepper, and 2 cups
wine. Cook over high heat until wine evaporates. Add the
water, tomato paste, and remaining wine; cover, and cook
over low heat 3 hours. Add potatoes and peas; cook 30
minutes longer. Taste for seasoning.

Serve with a dry red Bordeaux, a Burgundy like Beaujolais, a red Rhône wine like Châteauneuf-du-Pape, or a
dry red American wine.

Serves 6

RAGOUT DE QUEUE DE BOEUF
(oxtail stew)

2 2-pound oxtails, cut in	1/2 teaspoon thyme
serving-size pieces	4 tablespoons olive oil
3/4 cup flour	2 cups boiling water
2 teaspoons salt	3 cups dry red wine
1/2 teaspoon freshly	2 cloves
ground black pepper	12 small white onions

3 sprigs parsley	tied	3 carrots, cut in eighths
2 stalks celery	together	lengthwise
1 bay leaf	(bouquet garni)	4 potatoes, peeled and diced

1 clove garlic, minced
1 leek

1 cup sliced mushrooms

Pour boiling water over the oxtail pieces; drain and dry. Roll in a mixture of the flour, salt, pepper, and thyme. Heat the oil in a deep heavy casserole or Dutch oven, and brown the oxtails on all sides. Pour off the fat. Add the boiling water and wine. Stick the cloves in one of the onions. Add to the casserole with other onions, the bouquet garni, the garlic, and leek. Cover tightly, and bake in a 300° oven 2 1/2 hours. Add the carrots, potatoes, and mushrooms. Re-cover, and bake 1 hour longer. Skim fat off the top; taste for seasoning.

Serve with a red Bordeaux or Burgundy, or an American red wine.

Serves 6-8

TRIPPA ALLA FIORENTINA
(tripe in meat sauce)

2 pounds tripe	3/4 cup peeled, chopped
2 tablespoons butter	tomatoes
3/4 cup chopped onion	2 teaspoons salt
1/2 cup grated carrot	1/2 teaspoon freshly
1/2 pound beef	ground black pepper
(one piece)	1/2 teaspoon thyme
3/4 cup dry white wine	1/2 cut grated Parmesan cheese

Wash the tripe, cover with water, and bring to a boil; cook over low heat 1 hour. Drain, cool, and cut into strips 2 inches long and 1/2 inch wide. Meanwhile prepare the sauce.

Melt the butter in a saucepan; brown the onion, carrot, and beef in it. Add the wine, tomatoes, salt, and pepper; bring to a boil, cover, and cook over low heat 1 hour. Add the thyme and tripe; re-cover, and cook 1 hour longer. Remove the beef. Serve sprinkled with the cheese.

Serve with a dry American or German white wine, a light red Bordeaux, or a *rosé*.

Serves 6-8

CALF'S FOOT STEW

4 calf's feet	1 tablespoon salt
3 quarts water	1/2 teaspoon freshly
1 cup sliced onion	ground black pepper
3 sprigs parsley	1 cup chopped tomatoes
2 stalks celery	1 1/2 cups dry red wine
1 bay leaf	2 egg yolks

Have the feet chopped up, bone and all, into small pieces. Pour boiling water over them, and scrape the skin. Combine the feet with the water, onion slices, parsley, celery, bay leaf, salt, pepper, and tomatoes. Bring to a boil, and cook over low heat 3 hours. Remove the feet; cut the meat in small pieces discarding the bones. Mix the wine into the stock; cook over high heat 20 minutes. Return the meat; cook 10 minutes. Beat the egg yolks in a bowl; gradually add the hot mixture, stirring steadily to prevent curdling. Serve in deep bowls, with garlic toast.

Serve with any dry red wine, especially a Burgundy.

Serves 6-8

BRAISED KIDNEYS

1 pound veal kidneys	1 teaspoon grated lemon
3 cups boiling water	rind
2 tablespoons lemon juice	1/2 cup Marsala or sweet
4 tablespoons butter	sherry
1 1/4 teaspoons salt	3 tablespoons minced
1/4 teaspoon freshly	parsley
ground black pepper	

Wash the kidneys, cut in half, and remove the core. Soak in the boiling water mixed with the lemon juice for 3 minutes. Drain, then slice thin.

Melt the butter in a skillet; sauté the kidneys 5 minutes. Mix in the salt, pepper, lemon rind, and wine. Cook over medium heat 5 minutes. Sprinkle with the parsley.

Serve with a dry red Bordeaux or a Burgundy, especially a Beaujolais, a dry Italian red wine like Valpolicella, or an American red wine.

Serves 4

HASSENPFEFFER
(marinated rabbit)

2 rabbits (about 4 pounds)	1 tablespoon pickling
2 cups dry red wine	spice
1 cup wine vinegar	3 bay leaves
1 cup water	2 cups sliced onions
2 teaspoons salt	1/2 cup flour
3/4 teaspoon freshly	4 tablespoons butter
ground black pepper	1 tablespoon sugar
6 cloves	1 cup sour cream

Rabbits are available fresh and frozen. Have the rabbits cut in serving-size pieces. If frozen rabbits are used, thaw them partially. Place in pieces in a large glass or pottery bowl. Add a mixture of the wine, vinegar, water, salt, pepper, cloves, pickling spice, bay leaves, and onion slices. Cover and let marinate in the refrigerator 36 hours, basting and turning the pieces a few times.

Drain and dry the rabbit pieces. Reserve the marinade. Roll the rabbit in the flour. Melt the butter in a casserole; brown the rabbit pieces in it. Strain the marinade over the rabbit, and add the sugar. Bring to a boil; cover, and cook over low heat 45 minutes, or until tender. Taste for seasoning. If gravy is thin, stir 2 tablespoons flour, mixed with a little water, into the gravy, then gradually mix in the sour cream. Heat, but do not let boil.

Serve with a heavy Burgundy, especially a Beaujolais, a red Rhône wine like Châteauneuf-du-Pape, or any dry American red wine.

Serves 6

CARCIOFI ALLA ROMANA
(Roman-style artichokes)

6 small artichokes
2 cloves garlic, minced
1 cup minced parsley
1 teaspoon fresh mint,
    chopped, or 1/8
    teaspoon dried

2 teaspoons salt
1/2 teaspoon freshly
    ground black pepper
1/4 cup olive oil
1 cup dry white wine
1/2 cup chicken broth

Remove the tough outer leaves of the artichokes; cut off the sharp points of the remaining leaves. Carefully force the centers apart and cut out the chokes (furry centers). Mix together the garlic, parsley, mint, 1 teaspoon salt, and 1/4 teaspoon pepper. Stuff the centers of the artichokes. Arrange close together in a casserole; sprinkle with the oil. Cook over medium heat 10 minutes. Add the wine, broth, and remaining salt and pepper. Cover, and cook over medium heat 45 minutes, or until artichokes are tender.

Serves 6

JERUSALEM ARTICHOKES IN WHITE WINE

1 1/2 pounds Jerusalem
    artichokes
6 tablespoons butter
1/2 cup chopped onions
1 clove garlic, minced

3/4 cup dry white wine
1 teaspoon salt
1/8 teaspoon white
    pepper

Scrub the artichokes, pare, and dice. Melt the butter in a skillet; sauté the onion and garlic 5 minutes. Add the diced artichokes; sauté until lightly browned. Mix in the wine, salt, and pepper. Cover, and cook over low heat 15 minutes, or until tender.

Serves 4-6

HARICOTS VERTS PORTUGAISE
(green beans, Portuguese style)

2 slices salt pork or
    bacon, diced
1 cup peeled, chopped
    tomatoes
1 1/2 pounds green beans,
    or 2 packages frozen
    beans, thawed

1/2 cup dry white wine
1/4 cup beef broth
1 teaspoon salt
1/8 teaspoon white
    pepper
2 tablespoons minced
    parsley

Lightly brown the salt pork in a saucepan; pour off the fat. Add the tomatoes, beans, wine, broth, salt, and pepper. Bring to a boil; cover, and cook over low heat 30 minutes. Drain off most of the liquid. Taste for seasoning. Sprinkle with the parsley and serve.

Serves 6

BAKED BEANS IN WINE

3 cups dried white beans
1 1/2 teaspoons salt
1/2 pound salt pork
2 onions
4 cloves
2 cups dry white wine

1/3 cup dark rum
3/4 cup molasses
2 teaspoons dry mustard
1/2 teaspoon crushed
    dried red peppers

Wash the beans, cover with water, bring to a boil, and let soak 1 hour. Drain, add fresh water to cover, and the salt; bring to a boil, and cook over low heat 35 minutes. Drain.

Cut the salt pork into 1/2-inch cubes. Pour boiling water over it, and let soak 30 minutes. Drain.

Using an earthenware casserole, spread half the beans on the bottom. Cover with half the salt pork, the onions stuck with the cloves, then the remaining beans, and finally the remaining salt pork. Add a mixture of the wine, rum, molasses, mustard, and red peppers. Add enough boiling water to barely cover the beans. Cover casserole tightly and bake in a 250° oven for 4 1/2 hours, or until beans are tender, removing the cover for the last half-hour. Add a little boiling water from time to time during the first 4 hours to keep beans moist, but don't add any during the last half hour.

Serves 6-8

LIMA BEANS IN WINE SAUCE

2 packages frozen lima beans
1/2 cup sour cream
3/4 cup dry white wine
1/8 teaspoon white pepper
1/4 cup minced pimientos
2 tablespoons minced parsley

Cook the lima beans 1/2 minute less than package directs. Drain well. Mix together the sour cream, wine, and pepper. Add to the beans, with the pimientos. Cook over low heat 5 minutes, but do not let boil. Taste for seasoning. Sprinkle with the parsley and serve.

Serves 4-6

LIMA BEANS AND ONION CASSEROLE

4 tablespoons butter
18 small white onions, peeled
1 tablespoon flour
1 cup dry white wine
1 bay leaf
1/8 teaspoon thyme
1 teaspoon salt
1/8 teaspoon white pepper
2 cups shelled fresh lima beans, or 1 package frozen beans, thawed

Melt the butter in a casserole; sauté the onions until delicately browned. Stir in the flour and add the wine, bay leaf, thyme, salt, and pepper. Cover, and cook over low heat 15 minutes. Mix in the lima beans; cover, and cook over low heat 15 minutes, or until beans are tender. Shake the casserole occasionally to prevent burning. Taste for seasoning.

Serves 4-6

RED CABBAGE AND APPLES IN RED WINE

2 2-pound firm heads red
  cabbage
4 tablespoons butter
4 tart apples, peeled and
  quartered
1/2 cup chopped onion
1 1/2 teaspoons salt

1/4 teaspoon freshly
  ground pepper
2 cloves
1 bay leaf
2 tablespoons wine vinegar
1 1/2 cups dry red wine
2 tablespoons brown sugar

Wash cabbage, dry, and slice very thin, discarding the thick center core. Melt 2 tablespoons of the butter in a Dutch oven or heavy saucepan. Add the cabbage, apples, chopped onion, salt, pepper, cloves, bay leaf, vinegar, and red wine. Bring to a boil, cover, and cook over low heat 3 hours adding a little hot water during cooking, if necessary. Stir in the brown sugar and remaining butter; cook 5 minutes. Remove bay leaf and cloves.

Serves 6-8

CHOU AU CHAMPAGNE
(cabbage in champagne)

3 tablespoons butter
1 cup chopped onion
1 3-pound head cabbage,
  shredded
2 tablespoons flour
3/4 cup champagne or
  dry white wine

3 tomatoes, cut in eighths
1 1/2 teaspoons salt
1/8 teaspoon pepper
1 teaspoon sugar

Melt the butter in a saucepan; sauté the chopped onion and the cabbage 15 minutes, stirring frequently. Mix in the flour. Add the champagne, stirring constantly to the boiling point. Add the tomatoes, salt, pepper, and sugar. Cover, and cook over low heat 30 minutes.

Serves 6

CABBAGE IN RED WINE

4 pounds red cabbage
6 tablespoons butter

3 cups diced apples
1/2 cup chopped onion

1 1/2 teaspoons salt
3 cloves
1 bay leaf

2 cups dry red wine
2 tablespoons vinegar
3 tablespoons currant jelly

Shred the cabbage very fine. Melt the butter in a casserole or heavy saucepan. Add the cabbage, apples, onion, salt, cloves, and bay leaf. Mix lightly, then add the wine, vinegar, and jelly. Bring to a boil, cover, and cook over low heat 2 1/2 hours. Stir once or twice, and watch carefully to prevent burning. Discard bay leaf.

Serves 6-8

CHOUX–FLEURS BOURGUIGNON
(cauliflower in wine sauce)

3 tablespoons butter
1 tablespoon flour
1 teaspoon salt
1/8 teaspoon white
    pepper

1/2 cup dry white wine
1/2 cup heavy cream
1 medium cauliflower,
    cooked and drained

Melt the butter in a saucepan; stir in the flour, salt, and pepper. Add a mixture of the wine and cream, stirring steadily to the boiling point, then cook over low heat 5 minutes.

Place the cauliflower in a hot serving dish, and pour the sauce over it.

Serves 4-6

CELERY WITH CHAMPAGNE SAUCE

4 tablespoons butter
3/4 cup chopped onion
1 carrot diced
1/4 pound ham, diced
1/4 pound tongue, diced
2 tablespoons chopped
    parsley

1/2 teaspoon tarragon
1 bay leaf
3/4 cup champagne or
    dry white wine
1/2 cup chicken broth
3 bunches celery

Melt the butter in a saucepan; add the onion, carrot, ham, tongue, parsley, tarragon, bay leaf, champagne, and broth.

Bring to a boil cover, and cook over low heat 45 minutes.

Cut the leaves from the celery and remove the large outer stalks. Cut each bunch in half lengthwise. Add to the sauce; cover, and cook over low heat 15 minutes longer, or until the celery is tender. Taste for seasoning, and serve.

Serves 6

MUSHROOMS AND ARTICHOKES

4 tablespoons butter
2 packages frozen
    artichoke hearts,
    thawed
1 pound mushrooms,
    sliced

1 1/4 teaspoons salt
1/4 teaspoon freshly
    ground black pepper
1/4 teaspoon thyme
1/2 cup dry sherry

Melt the butter in a skillet; sauté the artichoke hearts 3 minutes. Add the mushrooms; sauté 2 minutes. Season with the salt, pepper, and thyme; add the sherry. Cook over high heat 5 minutes.

Serves 6-8

MUSHROOMS WITH FOIE GRAS

1 pound firm large white
    mushrooms
1 cup boiling water
3/4 teaspoon salt
2 teaspoons lemon juice
3 tablespoons butter

2 tablespoons chopped
    shallots or onion
1/4 cup finely diced ham
1 cup dry white wine
Foie gras

Wash the mushrooms and remove the stems. Chop the stems. Put caps in a saucepan with the boiling water, salt, lemon juice, and half the butter. Cover, and cook 3 minutes. Drain caps, and arrange in a buttered shallow baking dish, hollow side up. Melt the remaining butter in a skillet and sauté the shallots and ham 3 minutes; add the chopped stems; continue sautéing for 3 minutes over high heat. Add the wine, and cook over low heat 20 minutes, or until the mixture is fairly dry. Fill mushroom caps with stuffing, and put a thin slice of foie gras on each. Place in 425° oven for 5 minutes.

Serve with a dry red Bordeaux or Burgundy, or with a dry American wine.

Serves 4

MUSHROOMS SAUTÉED IN WINE

4 tablespoons butter
1 pound mushrooms, sliced
1 tomato, peeled and chopped
1 tablespoon chopped parsley

1/2 cup dry white wine
1 teaspoon salt
1/8 teaspoon freshly ground black pepper

Melt the butter in a skillet. Add the mushrooms, tomato, and parsley. Sauté 5 minutes, stirring frequently. Add the wine, salt, and pepper. Cook over high heat for 3 minutes, stirring frequently. Serve as a vegetable, or as an appetizer on toast.

Serves 2-4

CHAMPIGNONS BOURGUIGNON
(mushrooms with wine butter)

1 cup dry red wine
1 clove garlic, minced
3 tablespoons chopped green onion
1/4 pound (1 stick) butter
1/2 teaspoon freshly ground black pepper

1 tablespoon minced parsley
24 mushroom caps
3/4 teaspoon salt
4-6 slices hot buttered toast, trimmed

Cook the wine, garlic, and chopped onion until reduced to half. Cool. Cream the butter (reserving 2 tablespoons), then beat in the wine mixture, pepper, and parsley.

Melt the remaining butter in a skillet; sauté the mushrooms 5 minutes. Season with the salt. Arrange the mushrooms on the toast, hollow side up. Divide the wine butter among the mushroom caps. Serve at once.

Serves 4-6

GREEN PEPPERS IN WHITE WINE

4 tablespoons olive oil
2 cups coarsely chopped
    onion
4 cups julienne-cut green
    peppers
1 cup dry white wine

1 1/2 teaspoons salt
1/4 teaspoon freshly
    ground black pepper
2 tablespoons minced
    parsley

Heat the oil in a skillet; sauté the onion 10 minutes. Add the green peppers, wine, salt, and pepper. Cook over low heat 25 minutes, or until peppers are tender. Sprinkle with the parsley.

Serves 4-6

STUFFED GREEN PEPPERS

6 green peppers
3 tablespoons butter
1/2 pound mushrooms,
    coarsely chopped
3 tablespoons grated
    onion
1/4 pound ham, shredded
2 tablespoons tomato
    paste

4 tablespoons dry bread
    crumbs
3 tablespoons olive oil
3 tablespoons flour
1/4 cup beef broth
1 cup dry white wine

Cut a 1-inch slice from the stem end of the peppers. Cover the peppers with water; bring to a boil, and cook 5 minutes. Drain and cool.

Melt the butter in a skillet; sauté the mushrooms and grated onion for 5 minutes. Add the ham and 1 tablespoon of the tomato paste. Cook over low heat 5 minutes. Stir in the bread crumbs. Stuff the peppers with the mixture.

Arrange the peppers, stuffed side up, in an oiled baking dish. Sprinkle the olive oil over and around them. Bake in a 400° oven for 10 minutes. Mix together the flour, broth, wine, and remaining tomato paste. Pour over the peppers. Reduce heat to 350°, and bake 45 minutes longer, basting frequently. Taste for seasoning. Serve as an appetizer, or with roast meat or poultry.

Serve with a *rosé*, a dry American or German white wine, or a white Burgundy.

Serves 6

FESTIVE POTATOES

4 large potatoes, peeled
    and sliced as thin as
    possible
1 1/2 cups thinly sliced
    onions
2 teaspoons salt
1/2 teaspoon freshly
    ground black pepper

5 tablespoons butter
1/2 cup dry white wine
1/4 cup heavy cream
2 tablespoons dry bread
    crumbs
2 tablespoons grated
    Parmesan cheese

In a buttered 9-inch pie plate, arrange layers of sliced potatoes and onions, sprinkling each layer with salt and pepper, and dot with half the butter. Mix together the wine and cream, and pour over the top; sprinkle with the bread crumbs and cheese, and dot with the remaining butter. Bake in a 375° oven 45 minutes, or until the potatoes are tender. Serve in pie-shaped wedges.

Serves 4-6

CHOUCROUTE AUX CHAMPAGNE
(sauerkraut with champagne)

2 pounds sauerkraut
3 apples, peeled and
    sliced
1 teaspoon salt
1/2 teaspoon freshly
    ground black pepper

3 cloves
2 cups champagne
3 tablespoons butter

Wash the sauerkraut under cold running water. Drain very well.

In a buttered casserole, arrange alternate layers of sauerkraut and apples. Sprinkle with the salt and pepper, and add the cloves. Pour the champagne over it. Dot with the butter. Cover the casserole.

Bake in a 300° oven for 1 1/2 hours, or until the sauerkraut is tender, and almost all the liquid absorbed. Especially delicious when served with roast turkey or pork.

Serve with any dry white wine.

Serves 6-8

SAUCES AND DRESSINGS

BROWN SAUCE

1/4 cup minced shallots
    or onions
2 tablespoons butter
1 tablespoon flour
2 cups canned beef broth
2 teaspoons tomato paste

1 bay leaf
1/8 teaspoon freshly
    ground black pepper
1/8 teaspoon thyme

Sauté the minced shallots or onion in the butter for 5 minutes. Stir in the flour and cook over low heat, stirring frequently, until browned. Slowly mix in the broth, stirring steadily to the boiling point. Add the tomato paste, bay leaf, pepper, and thyme, and cook over low heat 20 minutes. Strain. Use as a base for other sauces, or serve on meats.

Makes about 1 1/2 cups

SAUCE DUXELLES
(mushroom sauce)

1 tablespoon olive oil
3 tablespoons butter
1/4 pound mushrooms,
    chopped fine
2 tablespoons chopped
    shallots or green
    onions
1/3 cup dry sherry

1 1/2 cups Brown Sauce
    (see recipe)
1 1/2 tablespoons tomato
    paste
3 tablespoons minced
    parsley

Heat the oil and 1 tablespoon butter in a saucepan; sauté the mushrooms and shallots 3 minutes. Add the sherry; cook over high heat until sherry is almost evaporated. Mix in the Brown Sauce, tomato paste and parsley. Cook over low heat 5 minutes. Taste for seasoning. Just before serving, blend in the remaining butter. Serve with chicken, veal, eggs, or *pasta*.

Makes about 2 cups

SAUCE ROUENNAISE

4 duck livers or 8 chicken
   livers
3 tablespoons minced
   onion
1 tablespoon butter

1/4 cup dry red wine
1 1/2 cups Brown Sauce
   (see recipe)
1 tablespoon cognac

Wash the livers carefully, removing any discolored areas.
Purée the livers in a blender; or chop, then force through
a fine sieve. Refrigerate until needed.

Sauté the minced onion in the butter 5 minutes. Add the
wine, and cook until reduced to half. Stir in the Brown
Sauce and cognac; cook over low heat 10 minutes. Just
before serving, mix 1/4 cup of the hot sauce with the liver.
Return to the balance of the sauce; heat, but do not let
boil. This is an extremely rich sauce. Serve with duck.

Makes about 1 3/4 cups

SAUCE LYONNAISE

1/4 cup minced onion
2 tablespoons butter

1 cup dry white wine
1 1/2 cups Brown Sauce

Sauté the minced onion in the butter 10 minutes. Add
the wine and Brown Sauce; cook over low heat 5 minutes.
Serve with game or beef.

Makes 2 cups

BORDELAISE SAUCE

Large marrow bone
2 tablespoons minced
   shallots or onion
1/4 cup dry red wine

1 cup Brown Sauce
   (see recipe)
1 tablespoon cognac
1 teaspoon minced parsley

Have the butcher crack the bone; carefully remove the
marrow. (You need about 3 tablespoons.) Dice it, and
place in lukewarm water for 5 minutes, then drain.

Cook the shallots and wine for 5 minutes. Stir in the Brown Sauce and cognac; cook over low heat 10 minutes. Add the marrow and parsley just before serving. Heat. Taste for seasoning. Serve with steak or roast beef.

Makes about 1 1/4 cups

SAUCE BIGARADE

1/2 cup boiling water
4 tablespoons grated
   orange rind
3 tablespoons minced
   shallots or onion
1/2 cup dry red wine
1 1/2 cups Brown Sauce
   (see recipe)

1/2 cup orange juice
1 tablespoon red currant
   jelly
2 tablespoons Grand
   Marnier or Curaçao

Pour the boiling water over the rind, and let soak 5 minutes. Drain.

Cook the shallots in the wine until wine is reduced to half; stir in the Brown Sauce, orange juice, jelly, and liqueur. Cook over low heat 10 minutes, stirring frequently. Add the orange rind. Serve with duck or game birds.

Makes about 2 cups

SAUCE FINES HERBES

2 teaspoons mixed dried
   herbs (tarragon,
   chervil, chives, thyme)
1/2 cup dry sherry
1 1/2 cups Brown Sauce
   (see recipe)

1/8 teaspoon lemon juice
2 teaspoons butter
1 tablespoon minced
   parsley

Cook the herbs and wine until wine is reduced to half; strain. Add to the Brown Sauce with the lemon juice. Cook over low heat 5 minutes. Stir in the butter and parsley until butter melts. Serve with eggs or fish.

Makes about 1 3/4 cups

SAUCE POIVRADE

2 tablespoons olive oil
1/3 cup minced onion
1/4 cup grated carrot
3 tablespoons minced
    parsley
1/2 cup dry red wine

1/4 cup wine vinegar
2 cups Brown Sauce
    (see recipe)
Dash ground cloves
1/4 teaspoon freshly
    ground black pepper

Heat the oil in a saucepan; sauté the onion, carrot, and parsley for 5 minutes. Add the wine and vinegar, cooking until liquid is reduced to half. Add the Brown Sauce; cook over low heat 30 minutes. Strain the sauce, and return to a clean saucepan; stir in the cloves and the pepper. Cook over low heat for 5 minutes. Serve with any game.

Makes about 2 1/4 cups

SAUCE VENISON

2 cups Sauce Poivrade
    (see recipe)
1 teaspoon lemon juice

3 tablespoons currant jelly
3 tablespoons heavy
    cream

Combine all the ingredients in a saucepan. Heat. Serve with venison.

Makes about 2 3/4 cups

SAUCE MADÈRE

3/4 cup Madeira or
    Amontillado sherry
2 teaspoons beef extract
1 cup Brown Sauce
    (see recipe)

1 tablespoon cognac
2 tablespoons butter

Cook the wine until reduced to half; stir in the beef extract and Brown Sauce. Cook over low heat 5 minutes. Add the cognac, and then the butter, stirring only until butter is melted. Serve with broiled meats or roast veal.

Makes about 1 1/2 cups

PERIGUEUX SAUCE

Sauce Madère (see recipe)   1/4 cup chopped truffles

Combine the Sauce Madère and truffles. Heat. Serve with pheasant, guinea hen, partridge, or beef.

Makes about 1 1/2 cups

SAUCE PORTUGAISE

2 tablespoons minced
  shallots or onion
2 tablespoons butter
1/2 cup dry red wine
1/2 cup peeled, diced
  tomatoes

1 cup Brown Sauce
  (see recipe)
1 teaspoon tomato paste

Sauté the shallots in the butter for 5 minutes. Add the wine, and cook until wine is reduced to half. Stir in the tomatoes, Brown Sauce, and tomato paste. Cook over low heat 15 minutes. Taste for seasoning. Serve with poultry or beef.

Makes about 1 1/2 cups

SAUCE CHASSEUR

3 tablespoons butter
1/2 pound mushrooms,
  sliced
4 tablespoons minced
  shallots or onion
1/2 cup dry white wine
1 1/2 cups Brown Sauce
  (see recipe)

2 tablespoons tomato
  paste
1/4 teaspoon freshly
  ground black pepper
1 tablespoon minced
  parsley

Melt 2 tablespoons of the butter in a saucepan; sauté the mushrooms 5 minutes. Add the shallots, and sauté 2 minutes longer. Stir in the wine, and cook over low heat until wine is reduced to half. Add the Brown Sauce, tomato paste, and pepper. Cook 5 minutes. Blend in the remaining butter and the parsley. Serve with chicken, veal, or beef.

Makes about 1 1/2 cups

BÉARNAISE SAUCE

3 tablespoons tarragon vinegar
3/4 cup dry white wine
2 peppercorns
1 tablespoon finely chopped shallots or onion
1 tablespoon finely chopped fresh tarragon, or 1 teaspoon dried
1 tablespoon finely chopped fresh chervil, or 1 teaspoon dried
3 egg yolks
1/2 teaspoon salt
1 cup melted butter
2 teaspoons minced parsley
Dash cayenne pepper

Combine the vinegar, wine, peppercorns, shallots, tarragon, the chervil in a sauce pan; cook over low heat until reduced to half. Beat the egg yolks and salt in a bowl; gradually add the wine mixture, beating steadily to prevent curdling. Gradually add the butter, beating steadily until the mixture is the consistency of very thick cream. Place over hot water, and beat for 1 minute. Strain, and add the parsley and cayenne pepper. If fresh herbs are used, add 1 teaspoon more of each before serving. Serve with beef or fish.

Makes about 1 1/2 cups

Variation:

SAUCE VALAISE

Add 1 teaspoon *glace de viande* or meat extract to the
Béarnaise Sauce. Serve with broiled chicken or eggs.

HOLLANDAISE SAUCE

1/4 pound (1 stick) sweet butter	1/4 teaspoon salt
	1 tablespoon lemon juice
4 egg yolks	2 tablespoons heavy cream

Divide the butter into 3 pieces. With a wooden spoon,
beat the egg yolks, salt, and lemon juice in the top of a
double boiler. Place over hot, not boiling, water. Add 1
piece of butter and cook, stirring constantly, until butter
melts. Add another piece of butter, and stir constantly
until butter is absorbed. Add the last piece of butter, and
stir until thickened. Be sure water does not boil.

Remove from the heat and blend in the cream. Serve
as soon as possible. Serve with fish or vegetables.

Makes about 1 1/4 cups

SALSA AMARILLA
(egg sauce)

6 hard-cooked eggs	1/4 teaspoon white pepper
1/4 cup sweet sherry	
2 tablespoons olive oil	1/2 teaspoon dry mustard
1 tablespoon white vinegar	2 tablespoons chicken broth or water
1/2 teaspoon salt	

Separate the yolks and whites of the eggs. Force the whites
through a sieve. Mash the yolks; mix in the sherry, then
the oil, drop by drop. Blend in the vinegar, salt, pepper,
mustard, broth, and egg whites. Serve with fish dishes.

Makes about 3/4 cup

SAUCE ESTRAGON
(tarragon wine sauce)

4 tablespoons butter
3 tablespoons flour
2 cups milk, scalded
1/2 teaspoon salt
1/4 teaspoon white
   pepper
1 cup dry white wine

3 tablespoons minced
   green onions
4 tablespoons minced
   fresh tarragon, or 1
   tablespoon dried
3 tablespoons minced
   parsley

Melt 2 tablespoons of the butter in a saucepan. Blend in
the flour, and cook, stirring over low heat until frothy. Do
not let brown. Remove from the heat and let stand until
mixture stops bubbling. Add the milk, beating with a wire
whisk. Cook over low heat, beating steadily to the boiling
point, then cook 5 minutes longer. Season with the salt
and pepper.

In a saucepan, combine the wine, minced green onions,
and tarragon. Bring to a boil and cook over medium heat
until reduced to about 3 tablespoons. Strain into the white
sauce; cook over low heat 2 minutes. Taste for seasoning.
Just before serving, blend in the remaining butter and the
parsley. (If fresh tarragon is used, add more tarragon in
place of the parsley.) Serve with fish, vegetables, eggs, or
chicken.

Makes about 2 cups

SUGO DI CARNE
(meat sauce with white wine)

3 dried mushrooms
2 tablespoons butter
3/4 cup chopped onion
1/2 cup grated carrot
3 tablespoons minced
   parsley
3/4 pound ground beef

1 tablespoon flour
1 1/2 teaspoons salt
1/2 teaspoon freshly
   ground black pepper
2 teaspoons tomato paste
1 1/2 cups dry white wine
1 cup beef broth

Wash the mushrooms, cover with water, and let soak 15
minutes. Drain and slice.

Melt the butter in a saucepan; sauté the onion, carrot, and parsley 5 minutes. Add the meat and mushrooms; cook over medium heat, stirring almost constantly until browned. Blend in the flour, salt, and pepper, then the tomato paste. Add the wine and broth. Cook over low heat 45 minutes, stirring frequently. Taste for seasoning. Serve with *pasta*, or use as a sauce for meat.

Makes about 3 cups

MEAT SAUCE (WITH RED WINE)

1 pound ground beef
2 tablespoons flour
4 tablespoons olive oil
3/4 cup chopped onion
1/4 cup grated carrot
3 tablespoons minced
    parsley
1 1/2 cups dry red wine
1 16-ounce can Italian-
    style tomatoes

1 1/2 cups beef broth
3/4 cup chopped
    mushrooms
1 1/2 teaspoons salt
1/2 teaspoon freshly
    ground black pepper
1/2 teaspoon basil

Toss the beef with the flour. Heat the oil in a saucepan; sauté the onion, carrot, and parsley 10 minutes. Add the beef; cook until browned, stirring frequently to prevent lumps from forming. Mix in the wine; cook over high heat 5 minutes. Add the tomatoes, broth, mushrooms, salt, pepper, and basil. Cook over low heat 1 1/2 hours. Taste for seasoning. Serve with *pasta* or with meat dishes.

Makes about 3 cups

SALSA DI FEGATINI
(chicken-liver sauce)

5 dried mushrooms
1 pound chicken livers
3 tablespoons flour
4 tablespoons butter
1 teaspoon salt
1/4 teaspoon freshly
    ground black pepper

1/2 cup Marsala or sweet
    sherry
1 1/4 cups chicken broth
2 tablespoons minced
    parsley

Wash the mushrooms, cover with warm water, and let soak 15 minutes. Drain and chop.

Wash the livers, remove any discolored areas, and dry. Dice the livers and toss with the flour.

Melt the butter in a saucepan; sauté the livers and mushrooms 5 minutes. Stir in the salt, pepper, and wine; cook over medium heat 5 minutes. Add the broth; cook over low heat 20 minutes. Mix in the parsley, and taste for seasoning. Serve with *pasta*, or use as a sauce for roast beef or steak.

Makes about 2 1/2 cups

SALSA ALLA GENOVESE
(Genovese sauce)

6 dried mushrooms (Italian, if available)	2 teaspoons salt
1/4 cup olive oil	1/2 teaspoon freshly ground black pepper
1 1/2 pounds ground chuck	2 bay leaves
3/4 cup chopped onion	2 cups dry red wine
2 cloves garlic, minced	1 6-ounce can tomato paste
1/2 cup chopped celery	2 cups hot beef broth
1/2 cup grated carrot	

Wash the mushrooms, cover with warm water, and let soak 10 minutes. Drain, and chop the mushrooms.

Heat the oil in a heavy saucepan; add the meat, and cook over high heat until browned, stirring frequently to prevent lumps from forming. Reduce heat; add the onion, garlic, celery, and carrot. Cook until browned. Mix in the mushrooms, salt, and pepper; cook 5 minutes. Add the bay leaves and wine, and bring to a boil. Stir in the tomato paste mixed with 1 cup of the broth. Cover, and cook over low heat 2 1/2 hours, adding some of the remaining broth from time to time. Taste for seasoning. Discard the bay leaves. Serve on any *pasta*, or as a sauce for roast meat.

Makes about 5 cups

RAGU
(Bolognese sauce)

2 tablespoons butter
1/4 pound ham, cut
    julienne
3/4 cup chopped onion
1/4 cup chopped celery
1/2 cup grated carrot
3/4 pound ground beef
1/2 pound chicken livers,
    diced

1 1/2 tablespoons tomato
    paste
1 1/4 cups dry white wine
1 cup water
1 teaspoon salt
1/2 teaspoon freshly
    ground black pepper
1/8 teaspoon nutmeg
1 cup heavy cream

Melt the butter in a saucepan; sauté the ham, onion, celery, and carrot 10 minutes, stirring frequently. Add the beef; cook over medium heat, stirring almost constantly, until browned. Stir in the livers; cook 2 minutes. Blend in the tomato paste, then stir in the wine, water, salt, pepper, and nutmeg. Cover, and cook over low heat 45 minutes, stirring frequently. Stir in the cream. Taste for seasoning. Serve with *pasta* or use as a sauce for meat.

Makes about 3 cups

ANCHOVY BUTTER SAUCE

1 tablespoon capers
1 tablespoon anchovy
    paste
1/4 cup dry sherry

1/4 pound butter
1 teaspoon lemon juice
2 teaspoons minced
    parsley

Rinse the capers under cold water; drain and chop.

Combine the anchovy paste with the sherry and butter in a saucepan; bring to a boil, and cook over low heat 10 minutes. Mix in the capers, lemon juice, and parsley; taste for seasoning. Serve with fish.

Makes about 3/4 cup

SHERRY–ROQUEFORT CHEESE DRESSING

1 egg
4 teaspoons sugar
1 tablespoon salt
5 cups salad oil
2/3 cup cider vinegar

1 clove garlic, minced
1/2 pound Roquefort
   cheese, diced
2/3 cup dry sherry

Beat the egg, sugar, and salt; gradually add the oil and half the vinegar, beating steadily. Stir in the garlic and cheese. Add the sherry and remaining vinegar, mixing until well blended. Chill until needed.

Serve on romaine, raw spinach, chickory, escarole, or a combination of greens. Be sure the greens are dry before adding dressing.

Makes about 1 1/2 quarts

DESSERTS

DEEP–DISH APPLE PIE

8 cups peeled, sliced apples	1 teaspoon cinnamon
2 tablespoons flour	1 tablespoon lemon juice
1/2 cup sugar	2 tablespoons butter
3/4 cup sweet sherry	Pastry for 1-crust pie

Toss the apples with the flour, and combine in a sauce-pan with the sugar, sherry, cinnamon, and lemon juice. Bring to a boil, and cook over medium heat 10 minutes. Drain almost all the liquid. Taste apples for sweetness, and add a little more sugar if necessary. Cool 10 minutes.

Spread the apples in a deep 9-inch pie plate. Dot with the butter. Roll out the pastry and cover the pie plate with it. Make a slit in the top. Bake in a preheated 400° oven 25 minutes, or until the pastry is golden brown. Serve warm or at room temperature.

Serve with a sweet American or German white wine, a sweet white Bordeaux, or with champagne.

Serves 6-8

FRAISES AUX CHAMPAGNE
(strawberries in champagne)

4 cups strawberries, washed and hulled	1 cup champagne
3/4 cup sugar	2 cups whipped cream
4 tablespoons kirsch (clear cherry brandy)	1/4 cup slivered blanched toasted almonds

Place the strawberries in a bowl. Sprinkle with the sugar. Toss lightly but throughly. Add 2 tablespoons of the kirsch, and the champagne. Chill for 2 hours.

Add the remaining kirsch to the whipped cream. Mix the strawberries in the bowl lightly, and divide among individual serving dishes. Cover with the whipped cream, and sprinkle the almonds on top.

Serve with champagne, a sweet Bordeaux, or a sweet German or American white wine.

Serves 6-8

CHERRIES IMPERIAL

2 cups fresh or canned pitted black sweet cherries	1 1/2 envelopes (1 1/2 tablespoons) gelatin
1/3 cup sugar	1 1/2 cups dry white wine
1/2 cup cognac	1 tablespoon lemon juice
	Blanched toasted almonds

Sprinkle the cherries with the sugar. (Use only 1/4 cup for canned cherries.) Cover, and chill 1 hour. Drain the juice into a measuring cup. Add the cognac and enough water to make 1 cup.

Soften the gelatin in 1/2 cup of the wine. Place over hot water, and stir until dissolved. Mix in the remaining wine, the cherry liquid, and the lemon juice. Using half the mixture, spoon into eight custard cups. Chill until set. Put an almond in each cherry and arrange over the set gelatin. Cover with the remaining gelatin mixture. Chill until set. Unmold, and serve with whipped cream.

Serve with champagne, a sweet white Bordeaux, a sweet German wine, or a sweet Italian white wine like Lacrima Christi.

Serves 8

PEACHES IN WINE SYRUP

2 pounds freestone peaches	1 tablespoon lemon juice
1/2 cup water	2 teaspoons grated lemon rind
1 1/2 cups dry white wine	Currant jelly
3/4 cup sugar	

Wash the peaches, plunge them into boiling water, then peel. Cut in half and discard the pits.

Bring the water, wine, and sugar to a boil. Add the

peaches, lemon juice, and rind. Cover, and cook over low heat 10 minutes, or until peaches are tender but firm. Remove the peaches and arrange in a serving dish, cut side up. Cook the liquid over medium heat until syrupy. Cool. Place a teaspoon of jelly in each peach half, and pour the syrup over them. Chill.

Serve with champagne, a sweet white Bordeaux, or a sweet American or German white wine.

Serves 6-8

STUFFED BAKED PEACHES

6 large firm freestone peaches	1 egg yolk, beaten
4 tablespoons butter	1 tablespoon cognac
2 tablespoons sugar	1 cup Marsala or sweet sherry
3/4 cup macaroon crumbs	

Peel the peaches, cut in half, and remove the pits. Scoop out a little of the pulp. Mash the pulp.

Cream the butter and sugar together; mix in the crumbs, peach pulp, egg yolk, and cognac. Stuff the peaches. Arrange in a buttered baking dish, and pour the wine over them. Pour the water into the dish. Bake in a 350° oven 25 minutes, or until peaches are tender but still firm.

Note: Canned cling peaches may be prepared in the same manner, but bake only 15 minutes.

Serve with a sweet white Bordeaux or with champagne.

Serves 6

AMBROSIA CUP

2 cups diced oranges	3/4 cup port
1 1/2 cups diced bananas	1 cup fine-grated coconut
1 cup diced pineapple	
3/4 cup sweetened pineapple juice	

Combine all the ingredients, and chill 1 hour before serving.

Serve with a sweet white Bordeaux, with champagne, or a sweet white American wine.

Serves 8-10

WINE BERRY MOUSSE

1 pint raspberries or
    strawberries
1 1/2 cups dry white wine
3/4 cup sugar
1 1/2 envelopes (1 1/2
    tablespoons) gelatin

1/4 cup water
1 cup heavy cream,
    whipped

Hull, wash, and drain the berries. Combine the wine and sugar in a saucepan. Cook over low heat, stirring steadily, until sugar melts. Add the berries. Bring to a boil again, then cook over low heat 1 minute. Drain the berries; return liquid to pan.

Soften the gelatin in the water, then stir into the hot liquid until dissolved. Add the berries. Chill until mixture thickens. Fold in the whipped cream. Turn into a lightly oiled 1 1/2-quart mold. Chill until set. Carefully unmold. Garnish with whipped cream and berries, if desired.

Serve with champagne, a sweet Bordeaux like Château d'Yquem, or a sweet American or German white wine.

Serves 6-8

CARAMEL APPLES

6 baking apples
1 1/3 cups packed brown
    sugar

6 tablespoons butter
1/3 cup dry white wine
2 tablespoons cognac

Wash and core the apples. Put a tablespoon of the brown sugar in each, then a tablespoon of butter. Arrange in a buttered baking dish.

Cook the wine, cognac, and remaining brown sugar 10 minutes, or until syrupy. Pour over the apples. Bake in a preheated 350° oven 35 minutes, or until apples are tender, basting frequently. Chill, Serve with whipped cream.

Serve with a sweet Bordeaux, or a sweet American or German or Italian wine.

Serves 6

BAKED APPLES IN WINE

6 large firm apples
6 tablespoons currant jelly
1 cup dry white wine

1/4 cup sugar
2 tablespoons butter

Peel and core the apples. Place a tablespoon of jelly in each. Arrange the apples in a baking dish. Mix the wine with the sugar, and pour over the apples. Dot with the butter. Bake in a 375° oven 35 minutes, or until the apples are tender, basting frequently. Serve hot or cold.

Serve with champagne, a sweet Bordeaux, or a sweet German wine.

Serves 6

BAKED STUFFED APPLES

4 tablespoons butter
1/2 cup packed brown
   sugar
1 teaspoon cinnamon

2 tablespoons cognac
1/2 cup chopped walnuts
6 large baking apples
3/4 cup sweet sherry

Cream together the butter and brown sugar until light and fluffy. Stir in the cinnamon, cognac, and nuts.

Wash the apples, remove the core, and peel about 2 inches down. Fill the centers with the nut mixture. Arrange in a buttered baking dish. Pour the sherry over the apples. Bake in a 375° oven 35 minutes, or until the apples are tender, basting frequently. Serve hot or cold, with whipped cream if desired.

Serve with champagne, a sweet American or German white wine, or a sweet white Bordeaux like Château d'Yquem.

Serves 6

APPLE HEDGEHOG

3 pounds apples
3/4 cup sugar
1/4 cup water
2 tablespoons lemon juice
1 envelope (tablespoon)
   gelatin

1/2 cup sweet sherry
3 drops red food coloring
1/2 cup sliced blanched
   almonds

Peel and core the apples, and cut in small pieces. Combine with the sugar, water, and lemon juice in a saucepan. Cook over low heat about 20 minutes, or until tender. Watch carefully to prevent scorching.

While the apples are cooking, soften the gelatin in the sherry. Stir into the cooked hot apples until dissolved. Purée in a blender, or force through a sieve. Taste for sweetness, and mix in the coloring.

Rinse a round or melon mold with cold water, and turn the apple mixture into it. Chill until firm. Unmold, and stud all over with the almonds.

Serve with champagne or a sweet Bordeaux.

Serves 6-8

POIRES AU VIN ROUGE
(baked pears in red wine)

8 firm pears
1 1/8 cups sugar

1 teaspoon vanilla extract
4 cups dry red wine

Peel the pears, but leave stem on. In a baking dish, mix together the sugar, vanilla, and wine. Arrange the pears in it. Cover the dish, and bake in a 350° oven 50 minutes, or until pears are tender but firm. Baste and turn pears frequently. Chill.

Serve with champagne, or a sweet German or American white wine.

Serves 8

PRUNE WHIP WITH PORT

1 pound unsweetened prunes	1 cup heavy cream
3/4 cup sugar	2 tablespoons confectioners' sugar
4 teaspoons cornstarch	1/4 cup slivered blanched almonds
1 cup port wine	

Wash the prunes, cover with water, and let soak overnight. Bring to a boil, add 1/2 cup of the sugar, and cook over low heat 25 minutes, or until prunes are tender. Drain, pit the prunes, and purée in a blender, or force through a sieve.

Return the prunes to the saucepan; add the cornstarch mixed with the wine and the remaining sugar. Cook over low heat, stirring steadily, until thickened. Cool.

Whip the cream, and fold half of it into the prune mixture. Turn into 6 serving dishes. Mix the remaining whipped cream with the confectioners' sugar, and spoon on top. Chill. Sprinkle with the almonds.

Serve with port wine, a sweet Bordeaux, or a sweet German or American wine.

Serves 6

PRUNE AND APRICOT COMPOTE

1 pound prunes	1/3 cup sugar
1/2 pound dried apricots	1 lemon, thinly sliced
2 cups dry white wine	1/2 cup blanched almonds
1 cup water	

Wash the prunes and apricots. Soak in the wine mixed with the water for 1 hour, then bring to a boil. Add the sugar and lemon. Cook over low heat 15 minutes, or until fruit is almost tender. Add the almonds; cook 5 minutes longer. Cool.

Serve with champagne, a sweet white Bordeaux, or a Loire Valley wine like Sancerre.

Serves 4-6

PLUM PUDDING

3 cups fresh fine bread
   crumbs
2/3 cup firmly packed light
   brown sugar
3/4 teaspoon salt
3/4 teaspoon cinnamon
1/2 teaspoon nutmeg
1/4 teaspoon ground
   cloves
3/4 cup dry red wine,
   heated
6 eggs, beaten
1/3 cup beef fat (suet),
   ground

1 cup seedless raisins
3/4 cup currants
1/4 cup chopped dates
1/4 cup chopped candied
   citron
1/4 cup chopped candied
   orange peel
1/4 cup chopped candied
   lemon peel
1/2 cup chopped apples
1/4 cup cognac

To make the bread crumbs, trim sliced white bread. Break the bread into small pieces and run in blender, or force through a sieve.

Mix the bread, brown sugar, salt, cinnamon, nutmeg, and cloves. Add the heated wine, and let stand 15 minutes. Mix in the eggs and suet. Using your hand, mix in the fruits and cognac. Be sure the fruits are well distributed.

Turn into a greased 2-quart mold. Cover tightly with the lid or with aluminum foil. Pour hot water to a depth of 1-inch into a pot with a cover. Place a rack in the pot and put the mold on it. Cover the pot, and cook over low heat 6 hours, adding boiling water from time to time to maintain the water level. The plum pudding may be served at once, or may be kept for a month or two. Reheat in the same manner before serving. Serve with hard sauce.

Serve with champagne, port wine, or sweet Bordeaux, or a sweet American or German wine.

Serves 10-12

ZABAIONE
(Marsala custard)

8 egg yolks
1/2 cup fine granulated
   sugar

1 cup Marsala or sweet
   sherry

Zabaione may be prepared at the table in a chafing dish or on the range in a double boiler. In the top part, beat the egg yolks and sugar with a wire whisk until thick. Beat in the wine; place over hot water and beat until hot and very thick, but do not let boil. Spoon into tall glasses or sherbert cups, and serve immediately. Serve with lady fingers, if desired.

Serve with champagne or a sweet American or Italian wine.

Serves 6-8

RICE–NUT DESSERT

1 1/2 cups raw rice
4 cups milk
1 teaspoon salt
3/4 cup Marsala or sweet
   sherry

3/4 cup sugar
3/4 cup ground almonds
3 egg yolks, beaten

Wash the rice under cold running water. Drain. Combine with the milk and salt; let stand 1 hour. Add the Marsala. Bring to a boil, and cook over low heat 15 minutes. Cool 10 minutes, then mix in the sugar, almonds, and egg yolks. Turn into a buttered baking dish. Bake in a preheated 350° oven 20 minutes. Chill.

Serve with champagne or a sweet white Bordeaux.

Serves 4-6

SHERRY BREAD SLICES

8 slices white bread
1 cup milk
2 eggs, beaten

4 tablespoons butter
1/2 cup honey
1/2 cup dry sherry

Trim the bread, and cut each piece in half. Soak in the milk 3 minutes, drain well, and dip in the beaten eggs.

Melt the butter in a skillet; lightly brown the bread in it. Arrange pieces in a buttered baking dish. Mix the honey with the sherry and pour over the bread. Bake in a 325° oven 20 minutes, or until glazed. Serve hot or cold.

Serve with a sweet American or German white wine, a sweet white Bordeaux like Sauternes, or a sweet Italian white wine.

Serves 4-6

CHAMPAGNE BAVAROIS

1 envelope (tablespoon) gelatin
2/3 cup champagne
4 egg yolks
3/4 cup sugar
1/8 teaspoon almond extract
1/2 cup ground blanched almonds
2 cups heavy cream, whipped

Soften the gelatin in the champagne. Place over hot water, and stir until dissolved.

Beat the egg yolks; add the sugar and almond extract, beating until thick and light in color. Gradually add the gelatin mixture, beating constantly. Mix in the almonds; fold in the whipped cream thoroughly but lightly.

Pour into a lightly oiled 2-quart mold. Chill until set, about 4 hours. Carefully unmold and serve. If desired, brandied fruits may be used as a garnish.

Serve with champagne, a sweet white Bordeaux, or a sweet American or German wine.

Serves 6-8

INDEX